MATT AND TOM OLDFIELD

ULTIMATE
FOOTBALL HEROES

LACAZETTE

FROM THE PLAYGROUND
TO THE PITCH

DINO

First published by Dino Books in 2020,
An imprint of Bonnier Books UK,
The Plaza,
535 Kings Road,
London SW10 0SZ

 @dinobooks
 @footieheroesbks
www.heroesfootball.com
www.bonnierbooks.co.uk

Design by www.envydesign.co.uk

Paperback ISBN: 9781789462449
E-book ISBN: 9781789462456

British Library Cataloguing-in-Publication Data:
A catalogue record for this book is available from the British Library.

Printed and bound in Great Britain by Clays Lltd, Elcograf S.p.A.

1 3 5 7 9 10 8 6 4 2

For all readers, young and old(er)

Matt Oldfield delivers sports writing workshops in schools, and is the author of *Unbelievable Football* and *Johnny Ball: Accidental Football Genius.* Tom Oldfield is a freelance sports writer and the author of biographies on Cristiano Ronaldo, Arsène Wenger and Rafael Nadal.

Cover illustration by Dan Leydon
To learn more about Dan visit danleydon.com
To purchase his artwork visit etsy.com/shop/footynews
Or just follow him on Twitter @danleydon

TABLE OF CONTENTS

ACKNOWLEDGEMENTS

First of all, I'd like to thank Bonnier Books UK – and
particularly my editor Laura Pollard – for supporting
me throughout and running the ever-expanding
UFH ship so smoothly. Writing stories for the next
generation of football fans is both an honour and a
pleasure.

I wouldn't be doing this if it wasn't for my brother
Tom. I owe him so much and I'm very grateful for
his belief in me as an author. I feel like Robin setting
out on a solo career after a great partnership with
Batman. I hope I do him (Tom, not Batman) justice
with these new books.

Next up, I want to thank my friends for keeping me sane during long hours in front of the laptop. Pang, Will, Mills, Doug, John, Charlie – the laughs and the cups of coffee are always appreciated.

I've already thanked my brother but I'm also very grateful to the rest of my family, especially Melissa, Noah and of course Mum and Dad. To my parents, I owe my biggest passions: football and books. They're a real inspiration for everything I do.

Finally, I couldn't have done this without Iona's encouragement and understanding during long, work-filled weekends. Much love to you.

CHAPTER 1

SAVING THE DAY IN THE NORTH LONDON DERBY

2 December 2018, Emirates Stadium

At half-time in the North London derby, things didn't look good for Arsenal. Their local rivals Tottenham were winning 2–1 and they weren't even playing that well.

Something had to change. Time for an Arsenal super sub, perhaps? That's what Alex was hoping as his teammates trudged into the dressing room. Because despite his exciting strike partnership with Pierre-Emerick Aubameyang, he was sat on the bench again.

Arsenal's manager Unai Emery had decided not to start the two of them together in such a tough derby match, but Arsenal were losing – they needed 'Auba' *and* 'Laca' out there in attack!

Thankfully, by half-time, Emery had changed his mind. 'Alex and Aaron,' he called out. 'Get ready, you're coming on.'

Alex's eyes lit up – he would have the full second half to save the day! Although he much preferred playing from the start, he had a great record as a super sub – first in the France national youth teams when he was younger, and then at Arsenal. With his pace, power and skill, Alex could cause problems for any defence.

Plus, he loved big games, and derbies in particular. One of his favourite football memories was scoring a hat-trick for his hometown club Lyon against their local rivals, Saint-Étienne. Now, he had the chance to be Arsenal's derby hero too.

In the tunnel, Alex pulled his socks up and put his gloves on. Then he looked over at Pierre-Emerick.

'Let's win this!' he said with a very serious look on his face.

As Auba and Laca walked out together for the

second half, the atmosphere in the stadium changed. Suddenly, the Arsenal supporters were hopeful again.

Come on, You Gunners!

Five minutes later, Aaron Ramsey raced forward from midfield and slipped the ball across to Pierre-Emerick, who curled a first-time shot into the back of the net.

Now Arsenal were level: 2–2 – game on! Arsenal attacked again and again, hunting for a winning goal. Sokratis missed a good chance, then Shkodran Mustafi, then Lucas Torreira. Oh dear – was the North London derby going to end in a disappointing draw?

No way, not while Alex was around! He tricked his way past Jan Vertonghen on the right wing and delivered a great cross towards Pierre-Emerick. It looked like a certain goal, but Juan Foyth got back just in time to head it away. Unlucky! Arsenal were getting closer and closer.

With fifteen minutes left, Aaron spotted Alex's run and played the perfect through-ball. On the edge of the penalty area, Alex paused to think. He had two defenders in front of him, and no-one to pass to. Oh well, he would just have to…

'Shoot!' the Arsenal fans urged. They knew how lethal their star striker could be.

BANG! Even though Alex struck it with his weaker left foot and slipped at the last second, his shooting accuracy was amazing. The ball skidded across the grass, past his old Lyon teammate Hugo Lloris, and into the bottom corner. *3–2!*

Goooooooooooooooooooaaaaaaaaaaaaaaaaalllllllllllll llllllllllllllll!!!!!!!!!!!!!!!!!!!

The Emirates Stadium exploded with noise and excitement. On the touchline, Emery threw his arms up in the air – what a double substitution! Alex was usually a calm, quiet character, but not after scoring such an important goal. He sprinted away from his teammates and then slid towards the corner flag on his knees.

Pierre-Emerick was the first to catch up with him. 'Laca, I love you, man!' he screamed in Alex's ear.

As they got back up, they did their special handshake together. With one arm behind their backs, they bowed at each other and then shook hands like old-fashioned gentlemen.

'Well done, sir!'

Alex had just saved the day for Arsenal in the North London derby. It was another unforgettable night for Lyon's favourite son.

CHAPTER 2

FAMILY LIFE IN LYON

Rose Lacazette loved her young family dearly, but she did enjoy the moments of peace and quiet when her four lively sons were outside playing their favourite sport – football.

Pass it!

Hey, that's a foul!

What a goal!

From their apartment on the thirteenth floor, Rose could still hear every loud kick and cry as the local kids battled below.

'They're football crazy, the lot of them!' she laughed to herself.

But at least her boys weren't out causing trouble in the centre of Lyon, the big, bustling city in the east of France where the Lacazettes lived. And they weren't fighting over the TV remote control at home either. No, she knew exactly where they were, and if she needed them, all she had to do was shout! Plus, hopefully, they would be nice and tired by the time they came back for dinner and then bed.

Hopefully. Every now and then, Rose went over to the window to keep an eye on her sons, and her youngest son in particular – Alexandre. He was still only five years old, but he was determined to do everything that his three older brothers did, especially when it came to football.

'Don't worry, Mum – we'll look after him!' Benoît promised as the four of them rushed downstairs after quickly dropping off their school bags.

But that didn't stop Rose from worrying. Alex was still very small, and he was shy too. What if he couldn't stand up for himself? She didn't want him to get hurt playing with bigger, stronger boys.

She needn't have worried, though. At home and in the classroom, Alex was often quiet and nervous, but he was like a completely different character once he stepped onto the tarmac football field. He felt much more comfortable there, especially when he had the ball at his feet and a goal in front of him. He loved football already and it helped that he was a natural.

'Woah, check out our wonderkid brother!' Benoît cheered as Alex skipped between two tackles and set up another goal for Raphaël.

'Yeah, if we don't up our game, he's going to be an even better player than the rest of us!' Jérôme warned with a smile.

The Lacazette brothers loved playing on the same team. Together, they could beat anyone, even if it was five players against the four of them! One day soon, they were all going to be the stars of their top local football team, Olympique Lyonnais. And then, who knew, maybe they would all win the World Cup for France too!

But even the greatest footballers on the planet needed to take an occasional break for food.

'BENOÎT, RAPHAËL, JÉRÔME, ALEX – DINNER TIME!'

'Coming, Mum!' they called back.

Then, amongst themselves, they called 'Same time tomorrow, yeah?' in agreement.

Rose listened to the noise getting louder and louder as her sons climbed the many, many stairs leading up to their apartment. By the time they reached the front door, they were almost out of breath. But they still greeted their mum with a stream of excited chatter, all four of them speaking at the same time:

'We won… *AGAIN!*'

'We haven't lost in weeks – we're so good it's getting boring!'

'You should have seen Alex today – he was awesome!'

Their father, Alfred, was back from work now, and he was also ready to hear all about their football adventures. When their dramatic tale finally came to an end, after many twists and turns, he gave his youngest son a big pat on the back. 'Well done, my boy – you're going to be a superstar!'

'Thanks Dad! What's for dinner? I'm sooooo hungry and it smells sooooo good!'

Their mother smiled. 'It's your lucky day, Alex. I cooked Chicken Colombo for you!'

Chicken Colombo was a super-tasty dish from Guadeloupe – an island in the Caribbean, which had once been part of France – and Rose had a special recipe because that's where her family was from.

'Yum, my favourite!' Alex cheered eagerly, almost drooling at the thought of it. First a fantastic football game, and then a delicious dinner – what a night!

Now that the Lacazette family was all together, it was definitely time for dinner. Well, almost.

'Right, the quicker you wash your hands, the sooner we can all eat it.'

'Yes, Mum!' her four sons called out as they raced each other to the bathroom.

Alex couldn't keep up with his bigger, stronger brothers, but he didn't mind losing this time. Because out on the football pitch, his winning days were just beginning.

CHAPTER 3

WORLD CUP 1998

France 3 South Africa 0,
France 4 Saudi Arabia 0,
France 2 Denmark 1...

With each World Cup win, the excitement was building all across the country. Everywhere you looked, there were blue, white and red French flags flying high. Could the national team go all the way and lift the Jules Rimet Trophy for the first time ever, in front of a loud, proud, home crowd?

In a certain thirteenth floor apartment, the whole family had caught World Cup fever, even Rose.

Allez Les Bleus! Allez Les Bleus!

It was an especially exciting time for the people of Lyon. Because not only was their local hero, Youri

Djorkaeff, playing a key role in midfield, but France's win over Denmark had taken place at the Stade de Gerland in Lyon. The stadium was close enough to the Lacazettes' tower block that the family could hear the cheers as each goal went in.

'Listen to that – we must have scored again!'

France were now through to the Round of 16, where they would face Paraguay. Could they keep their winning run going? The Lacazette brothers certainly believed in *Les Bleus*.

'Of course we can win the World Cup!' Benoît argued passionately. 'We've got the best defence in the whole tournament. We've only let in one goal so far and that was a penalty!'

'Plus, we've got Zizou in attack,' mentioned Raphaël, Zinedine Zidane's biggest fan.

'Hey, don't forget about Youri!' Jérôme reminded the others.

'*And* the best player of all,' Alex added, 'Henry!'

After watching him star in the group stage games, Thierry Henry was Alex's new favourite footballer. He was a speedy, skilful forward and he was still only twenty years old. Whenever their Number 12 was on the pitch, France looked way more dangerous.

Henry won the ball, nutmegged a South Africa defender and then coolly chipped it over the keeper. *GOAL!*

Henry sprinted into the six-yard box and beat the last Saudi Arabia defender to the ball. *GOAL!*

Henry pounced on another mistake by Saudi Arabia and raced through to score again. *GOAL!*

'He's sooooo good,' Alex marvelled out loud as he watched the replays on TV. 'I want to be just like him when I'm older!'

Alex was still only seven years old, but it was good to have a target to aim for.

There was one other reason why he loved Henry, and the whole of the new national team, in fact. That's because lots of the players had families who had arrived in France from other French-speaking countries, just like the Lacazettes had done.

Their star defender Marcel Desailly had been born in Ghana in Africa, and their midfield maestro Patrick Vieira had been born in Senegal.

Plus, Zidane's parents had come from Algeria, and best of all, Henry's father had come from... Guadeloupe!

'Hey, that's where Mum and Dad are from too!'

Alex celebrated that news even more enthusiastically than he celebrated Henry's goals. It was so cool to have a real connection with his football icon. He really could be just like his hero when he was older! It made him even more desperate to see Henry and his teammates do well at the World Cup.

Allez Les Bleus! Allez Les Bleus!

It wasn't easy, though, being a big France fan. Alex struggled to sit still as *Les Bleus* struggled to score past Paraguay. But eventually, in extra time, Laurent Blanc banged in the winner. *Phew!*

Allez Les Bleus! Allez Les Bleus!

The quarter-final against Italy was even harder to watch. Alex saw the penalty shoot-out through his fingers, but eventually, Laurent Blanc banged in the winner. *Phew!*

Allez Les Bleus! Allez Les Bleus!

Just when Alex thought things couldn't get any more nerve-wracking, France then went 1–0 down against Croatia in the semi-finals. Nooooooo! Was their World Cup dream about to end?

No way, because France were a brilliant, fearless team, and they had thousands of home fans cheering them on. There was no way they were giving up until the final whistle. The forwards weren't firing, so the right-back Lilian Thuram raced forward instead and scored two great goals. *Phew!*

Allez Les Bleus! Allez Les Bleus!

What an incredible comeback – France were through to the World Cup final!

'Guess where Thuram was born, boys?' Alfred asked his sons proudly. But before they could guess, he gave them the answer: 'Guadeloupe!'

Amazing! When the big day arrived, the Lacazette family settled down in front of the TV, ready to cheer on their favourite players.

'You can do it, Zizou!'

'We love you, Youri!'

'Go on, Lilian!'

Unfortunately, Henry was on the bench for the final, but Alex wasn't too disappointed. Hopefully, he would be able to come on in the second half and be the super sub who won the game.

This was going to be France's most difficult match yet, because they were up against Brazil, the four-time World Champions, who had lots of experience at the back, and in attack could boast a superstar strikeforce of Rivaldo and Ronaldo. Even a deadly defence like France's was going to find it hard to keep those two quiet.

'Come on, France!'

As the game kicked off at the Stade de France in Paris, a nervous silence fell over the Lacazette family in Lyon. Were *Les Bleus* strong enough to beat a team like Brazil? Or would their heroes fall apart in the final? It would be so disappointing to get so close to glory and yet not lift the golden trophy...

France's nervous silence lasted until the twenty-seventh minute. Emmanuel Petit curled a corner into the Brazilian box, and Zizou made a great late run to meet it. He headed the ball powerfully down into the bottom corner. 1–0 to France!

Hurraaaaay!

While the players celebrated on the pitch in Paris, the Lacazettes did the same in their living room. Alex jumped up on the sofa and threw a cushion into the air.

'We're going to do this,' he declared confidently. 'We're going to win the World Cup!'

He was right about that, and in the end, France made it look easy.

Youri crossed the ball and Zizou headed it past the keeper again. *2–0!*

Patrick passed to Emmanuel, who fired a shot into the bottom corner. *3–0!*

France were the new World Champions! That night, as he watched the captain Didier Deschamps lift the trophy high above his head, Alex cried tears of pure joy. He couldn't help it – he was so proud of all the France players, his football heroes.

'What an amazing feeling that must be!' Alex thought to himself as he watched them parade the World Cup around the pitch in front of all the celebrating fans.

Then he turned to look at his brothers. They were all sitting there, thinking the same thing:

'How cool would it be if we all won the World Cup together one day?'

CHAPTER 4

ELAN SPORTIF

So, what was Alex waiting for? If he wanted to be a World Cup winner one day, the first thing he needed to do was join a football club. Luckily, there was one just across the street from their apartment, where his brothers already played: Elan Sportif. It wasn't a smart, fancy football club like Lyon, but it was a good, friendly place to start. Plus, Rose would still be able to keep an eye on her youngest son from their window. Perfect!

As soon as Alex was old enough, Alfred signed him up for training sessions.

'Ah, the littlest Lacazette,' said one of Elan Sportif's youth coaches. 'Welcome, we've heard great things about you!'

The coaches already knew Alex because he was often there at the club, kicking a ball around while his dad watched his brothers. Now, it was his turn to play too! Alex couldn't wait to show off the skills that he had been practising for ages in their five-a-side games. If he could beat the bigger boys on the estate, then surely, he would be amazing against players his own age.

'Wow, look at that ball control!' Jean-Pierre Parsi thought to himself as he watched Alex in action for the first time. While he dribbled through the cones, the football stayed stuck to the boy's foot like a faithful companion.

The experienced Elan Sportif coach knew exactly what to look for in a promising young player, and Alex ticked all the right boxes. He had speed, skill *and* strength; he could pass, he could dribble, *and* he could shoot. In terms of talent, he certainly stood out from the rest.

But there was a lot more to football than just fancy footwork. To become a top player, you needed drive and determination. Well – growing up with three football-mad older brothers, Alex certainly had those attributes. Parsi could already see that the youngster worked harder than anyone else on the pitch. And although he didn't say very much, he was always listening, and he learned new things very quickly. That desire to improve was so important in a young footballer.

'That's it – excellent!' Parsi clapped and cheered.

Alex looked up and gave an embarrassed little nod. Hopefully, he wouldn't be so shy once he got used to his new Elan Sportif teammates…

'Yes, Danny – pass it!' Alex called out as he sprinted forward on the attack, a blur of red on the run. He just loved being on the ball, as often as possible.

After only a few weeks at the club, Alex was already feeling more comfortable and confident, just as Parsi had predicted. And he was scoring lots and lots of goals too.

He dribbled past one defender, then another, and then nutmegged the keeper. *GOAL!*

He flicked the ball around his marker and then

chased after it. *GOAL!*

He played a one-two with his teammate and then fired a shot into the top corner. *GOAL!*

The opposition defenders just didn't know what to do – once he started scoring, Alex was simply unstoppable! Unless…

'Coach, can I go in goal now – please?' he asked once Elan Sportif were winning 4–0, and he had his hat-trick. Alex loved scoring, but he didn't like showing off. Three was enough for him; it was someone else's turn to get the glory now. He wanted to play his other favourite position.

'Okay,' Parsi agreed, 'but only for a bit!'

'Thanks, Coach!'

Phew! The defenders breathed a big sigh of relief. Alex wouldn't be troubling them, at least for a little while.

Alex was a very good goalkeeper, flying through the air to make supersave after supersave. But the problem was that Elan Sportif often struggled when their star player wasn't out there shining on the pitch.

Without him, there was no-one who could take control of the game, no-one who could link up all the neat passing, and no-one who could dribble past three or four defenders to score a wondergoal whenever he liked.

Whenever Elan Sportif conceded a few goals and things started to look bad, Parsi would just put Alex back up front:

'We need you out on the field now!'

'Okay, Coach!'

He raced forward with the ball stuck to his right foot, weaving through his opponents until he could see the target in front of him. Time to shoot: *BANG! GOAL!*

'That's my boy!' Alfred clapped and cheered proudly on the sidelines. All four of his sons were talented footballers, but the youngest looked like he might be the best of the bunch.

For a long, successful time, Alex was Elan Sportif's star player in both positions. One day, however, he was forced to make a difficult decision.

'Goalkeeper?' Rose repeated in shock when she

found out about her son's second role. Alfred had managed to keep it a secret for ages, but now the truth had slipped out. 'No, no, no, Alex, you can't be doing that – it's far too dangerous!'

'But Mum, I love making saves!' he pleaded.

'No, I'm sorry, son,' Rose stood firm. 'From now on, you either play as a striker, or not at all.'

Alex was sad to say goodbye to goalkeeping, but he had no choice. He couldn't stop playing football altogether, could he?

'Don't worry, we'll just focus on turning you into an even better attacker now,' Parsi told his young player excitedly.

Alex really liked the sound of that. As he got older, he became more and more obsessed with scoring as many goals as possible for Elan Sportif. Often, he played as a midfield rather than a striker, but still every season, Alex's goal tallies went higher and higher:

Fifty,
Sixty,
Seventy…

… all the way up to 122!

Even while breaking local Lyon records, though, Alex still wasn't satisfied. If he missed a good chance in a game, he would stay angry about it for days.

'Why didn't I just take my time? That was such an easy finish!'

'Hey, we all make mistakes,' Parsi had to remind him at training. 'All you can do is learn from them and try to do better next time.'

And if Alex ever went a whole match without scoring, he would cry and cry.

'It's okay, you didn't let anyone down,' his Elan Sportif coach tried to comfort him. 'Even the top strikers on TV have tough games sometimes!'

The next week, Alex would bounce back stronger than ever, and score a brilliant hat-trick – or even more. Yes, even at that young age, he already had the winning mentality that would make him a star.

CHAPTER 5

SCOUTED BY LYON

Elan Sportif knew that they would lose their star player eventually. Sadly, they were only a small, local football team, and it was only a matter of time before a bigger club came along and asked Alex to join their academy. But which one would it be?

Would it be AS Lyon-Duchère, who played in the lower leagues of France?

Would it be AS Saint-Étienne, who played in Ligue 1, but were an hour's drive away?

Or, best of all, would it be Olympique Lyonnais, Alex's favourite team?

Lyon had just won the French league title for the last two seasons in a row – 2001–02 *and* 2002–03. Alex especially loved watching them play because they had so many amazing, exciting attackers: Brazilian playmaker, Juninho Pernambucano, who fired in lots of fantastic free kicks; French forwards, Péguy Luyindula and Sidney Govou, who loved to show off their speed and skill; and, best of all, Brazilian striker, Sonny Anderson, who scored lots and lots of goals.

Alex had always dreamed of becoming Lyon's 'next big thing', and not just because they were his favourite team who played close to his home. It was also because the club was famous for giving their young players a chance.

Their nickname was 'Les Gones', which meant 'The Kids' in the local language. Govou had started out in the Lyon academy, and so had defender Jérémie Bréchet and midfielders Florent Balmont and Alexandre Hauw. So, if Alex wanted to become a superstar striker like his hero Henry, Lyon would be the perfect place to be!

Alex was twelve years old now, and growing bigger, stronger and better at football all the time. He just needed an opportunity to show the Lyon youth coaches what he could do…

At that time, Gérard Bonneau had just taken over as their new Head of Youth Recruitment. It was a fancy title, which meant that it was his job to find talented young players who could one day become Lyon's stars of the future.

Bonneau had contacts at youth clubs all over the city, who were constantly calling up to tell him about the top new kid to look out for.

'Seriously, this guy's going to be the next Zidane!'

'He's got everything you'd want in a defender. He reminds me of a young Marcel Desailly.'

The difficult part for him, as a scout, was trying to work out which players would still stand out when they were eighteen years old, and which players would fade away into the 'quite good' category.

One of the many names mentioned to Bonneau was Alexandre Lacazette, an attacker for Elan Sportif, who had just scored 122 goals in one season.

'Wow – with a record like that, he's definitely worth a watch!' Bonneau decided. So off he went to see him in action.

Alex was supposed to be playing as an attacking midfielder that day, but really, he was playing all over the pitch. He battled for the ball in his own half, and then he dribbled it forward into the opposition half to launch the attack. He played clever passes to the teammates around him, and then he raced into the penalty area to finish off the move himself. *GOAL!*

'Interesting!' Bonneau thought to himself. What impressed him most was Alex's all-round ability. Not many young forwards were blessed with pace, power, touch *and* vision. It was a winning combination, especially when you added in goals as well.

'One thing's for sure,' Lyon's Head of Youth Recruitment said to himself as Alex jogged back to the halfway line without much of a celebration. 'This guy is too good to be playing at this level!'

There was something special about the boy, even if Bonneau couldn't quite explain it. Although he wasn't much of a talker on the pitch, Alex played the game with a quiet confidence, that said, 'I know what I'm doing, and I'm only just getting started!'

That was exactly what Bonneau was looking for – a young player with lots of natural football talent, but who still had plenty more developing to do. With the right coaching and support, who knew how good this kid could be? He certainly had a good chance of achieving his Ligue 1 dreams at Lyon.

Once the game was over and Elan Sportif had secured yet another victory, Bonneau went over to introduce himself to Parsi. Then, after a quick chat with the coach, he walked away in the direction where Parsi was pointing.

'Hi there, I understand you're Alex's dad?' he asked.

Alfred nodded. 'That's me! And you are?'

'My name is Gérard Bonneau, and I'm Lyon's Head of Youth Recruitment.'

Alfred raised his eyebrows at the sound of the 'L-word', but he let Bonneau continue.

'It's nice to meet you. You must be very proud of your son – what an exceptional young player he is! That's why I would like to offer him the opportunity to come and train at the Lyon academy. Do you think he would be interested in that?'

'Of course he would!' Alfred thought to himself, but he wasn't going to reply on his son's behalf. No, that wouldn't be fair. He wouldn't push Alex to play professional football; it had to be what *he* wanted to do.

'Mr Bonneau, why don't you ask him yourself. Alex?' Alfred called out across the field.

He was talking to his teammates, but he came straight over.

'Son, this is Gérard Bonneau – he works for Olympique Lyonnais.'

Woah! Suddenly, Alex's whole body was shaking with excitement. He was shy around most new people, plus this wasn't just any old new person – it was someone who worked for *Lyon.*

'Hi Alex, great game today! I was wondering if you'd like to come along and train at our academy? No pressure! If you like, we could start with a few trial sessions and see how that goes. Then if you enjoy it, we could talk about signing you up for next season.'

But Alex's mind had stopped listening at the 'train at our academy' part. At last – this was the big opportunity that he had been waiting for! To become Lyon's next big thing.

'Yes please, Mr Bonneau!' Alex managed to splutter out eventually.

'Great, but please call me Gérard!' Lyon's Head of Youth Recruitment replied with a laugh.

CHAPTER 6

HENRY AND THE ARSENAL INVINCIBLES

The 2003–04 season was a big one for Alex, his first at Lyon's famous football academy. But it was an even bigger season for his number one football hero.

Thierry Henry had made the move from Juventus to Arsenal back in 1999, not long after France's amazing World Cup win. Almost as soon as he arrived in England, he became a Premier League superstar, but he just kept getting better and better.

And so did Arsenal. By 2003, their manager Arsène Wenger had put together an invincible team. 'The Gunners' loved to play beautiful passing football, but they also worked hard to win every game. They had strength at the back and skill in attack. Talent plus determination, flair plus leadership – that was Alex's idea of perfection.

So now he had a favourite French team – Lyon – and a favourite English team too – Arsenal. Oh well, he would just have to watch even more football then! And in case Alex needed another good reason to support them, The Gunners had more than just that one fantastic Frenchman. There was also Patrick Vieira winning the ball in midfield, Robert Pires dribbling down the left wing, Sylvain Wiltord causing chaos in attack, and, of course, Wenger coaching the team on the touchline.

They were all Alex's heroes now, but Henry was still Number One, and he always would be. Because when Arsenal needed a moment of magic to win the match, their Number 14 was so often the star of the show.

The top-corner rocket against Manchester City, the curling free kick against Manchester United, the cool penalty chip against Newcastle, the heroic hat-trick against Liverpool, the fantastic four against Leeds United… Henry was a total football genius!

He played with such calm, such confidence, such creativity.

Alex loved watching Henry's goals again and again on TV. He sat as close to the screen as he could without his mum telling him off; he didn't want to miss a single touch of the ball. Then once he had learnt everything there was to learn, he would rush outside to try to copy his France and Arsenal hero.

Henry gets the ball on the edge of the box, he beats one defender, then another... GOOOAAALLL!!! What a beauty!

Alex threw his arms out to the side and raced along the wall, shouting at each brick as if they were the supporters at Highbury. Maybe one day if he kept working hard at Lyon, he too would be lighting up the Premier League for Arsenal.

But for now, it was all about Henry, the best striker in the business. He just kept on scoring that season – *twenty-five, twenty-six, twenty-seven...* – and Arsenal just kept on winning. At the end of the season, Henry was the Premier League's top scorer with thirty goals and the Player of the Year, and

Arsenal were the new Champions of England.

'Hurraaaaay!' Alex cheered all the way from France.

And that wasn't Arsenal's only amazing achievement of the season. They finished with a record of thirty-eight games played, twenty-six wins, twelve draws, and zero defeats.

That's right, 'The Invincibles' hadn't lost a single league game all season! That hadn't happened in English football since Preston Northern End in 1889, 115 years earlier. Alex was so proud of the Arsenal team, and especially his fellow Frenchmen. Their Premier League record was even more impressive than his 122 goals in one season for Elan Sportif.

'Anything Henry can do, I can do too!' he told himself, feeling inspired.

First the 1998 World Cup, and then the 2003–04 Invincibles; Alex now had big dreams to achieve for both club and country.

CHAPTER 7

ACADEMY LIFE AT LYON

From the moment Alex arrived at the Lyon academy, all the coaches could see his quality. His close control was excellent, and so was his burst of speed to escape from his marker. He read the game well and he was good in front of goal.

Those were the positives, so what about the negatives? Well, Alex wasn't as selfish as many young strikers. He preferred to pass and link up the play, rather than shooting every time from any angle. Plus, he didn't loudly demand the ball like some of his teammates. That wasn't his style and he wasn't going to pretend to be someone else. Instead, he just quietly got on with his natural game.

'He's brilliant, but does he really have that desire

to be the best?' some of the Lyon youth coaches wondered.

Bonneau nodded his head firmly. 'Yes, he does! Don't let that face fool you – Alex is far more determined than you think.'

He had to be, if he wanted to become a star at the Lyon academy. Alex wasn't just skipping across the street to play for Elan Sportif anymore. No, now he had to rush out of school to get the bus to the Tola Vologe training centre, where he was competing against the best young players in the city. And he often didn't arrive home again until after nine o'clock at night. Although Rose would have dinner waiting on a plate for him, Alex was sometimes too tired to eat by then.

'Sorry, Mum, all I want to do is sleep!'

Still, there was one good thing that Elan Sportif and the Lyon academy had in common – fun, attacking football. Alex's new coaches wanted to win, but they wanted to win 'the Lyon way'. That meant lots of passing and lots of movement. Making the odd mistake didn't matter, just so long as you were trying to play 'the Lyon way'.

Fortunately, that was exactly the way that Alex wanted to play – like Henry and the Arsenal Invincibles! He didn't want to just stand up front and finish things off; that was so boring, and he was too good a footballer for that. Instead, he wanted to be on the ball as much as possible, getting involved in all the fantastic, flowing build-up too.

'Yes, Yannis – one-two!'

'Here, I'll flick it on for you, Clément!'

The longer Alex spent at the Lyon academy, the more comfortable he felt there, and the better he became at football. He did miss Parsi and all his friends at Elan Sportif, but now he was working with some of the best youth coaches in the whole of France. They had so many interesting ideas about how Alex could improve as a player, and as a striker.

'Next time you're in that position, try making this run instead.' They showed him by drawing arrows on the white board. 'That way you'll draw the defender out and create space for Clément to move into.'

'Nice, I hadn't thought of that. Thanks, Coach!'

Alex was learning so much at the academy. Before, he had just seen football as a fun game where you could show off your skills and score great goals. But now that he was a teenager, he was starting to think more seriously about the sport. It turned out that there was a lot more to it than that. He needed to pay more attention to the little details, especially when it came to his decision-making:

Was that the best run to make?

What if I had passed that left instead of right?

Should I have taken that shot earlier?

Would I have scored that one if I'd gone for full power instead of placing it?

Alex knew that he had to get these things right if he wanted to become a star in the Lyon senior squad one day. That was the dream of every single academy player, but only a few of them at most would be lucky enough to make it. Although Alex was very talented, so were lots of his teammates. This wasn't Elan Sportif anymore, where he could be the star player without even trying that hard. If he didn't shine, then other players would:

Clément Grenier was a clever attacking midfielder with amazing technique and creativity.

And Yannis Tafer was a speedy winger with lots of tricks and a wicked shot.

Together, they formed an awesome attacking trio in the academy, but could they really all make it into the Lyon first team? The chances were slim, but if they carried on improving, anything was possible. After all, Karim Benzema and Hatem Ben Arfa had come through the academy together a few years earlier, and now they were both Ligue 1 stars for Lyon.

'That could be us next, lads!'

Alex just had to keep believing in himself and keep challenging himself alongside Clément and Yannis. To become the best, he had to compete against the best.

CHAPTER 8

FUTURE OF FRANCE PART 1

Alex, Clément and Yannis were in high spirits as they waved goodbye to their families at the airport.

'Turkey, here we come!' they cheered together. 'Sun, sea and football – what could be better than that?'

Lyon's brightest young things were now France's brightest young things too. They were off to represent their country at the 2008 Under-17 European Championships.

Five games in twelve days – it was going to be lots of hard work, and not much of a holiday. But Alex couldn't wait to challenge himself against the best young players from countries like Switzerland, Spain and the Netherlands. If he performed well, he could make a real name for himself, like Wayne Rooney had in 2002, and like Cesc Fàbregas had in 2004.

That year, France had won the tournament, thanks to Lyon's own Ben Arfa and Benzema. But every year since then, *Les Bleus* had failed to reach the final.

'But now we're here to save the day!' Yannis declared confidently.

Yes, that was the plan. As well as Lyon's star trio, France also had Gilles Sunu and Gaël Kakuta, two wonderkids who had already signed for Arsenal and Chelsea. With so many amazing attackers in one squad, they were all set to take the trophy home.

But surely they couldn't all start in the same team, could they? In France's first match against the Republic of Ireland, the coach Francis Smerecki picked four of them to play: Clément, Yannis, Gilles and Gaël. Sadly, Alex was the one who was left on the subs bench.

'Never mind,' he thought to himself as he sat down to watch the first half with the rest of the squad. 'When I come on, I'll just have to show the boss that he made a big mistake!'

At half-time, France – with no Alex on the pitch – were losing 1–0. Alex kept looking across at his manager, but Smerecki wasn't ready to make a change just yet…

'Come on, Coach – pick me, I promise I'll score!' Alex said to himself, shaking his restless legs.

At last, as the minutes ticked away, his manager called for him. Alex jumped up out of his seat in a flash and then raced out onto the pitch. He didn't have much time to be the super sub.

With his friend now with him on the pitch, Yannis finally found his magic touch. He dribbled his way through the Irish defence and scored a beauty. *1–1!*

Now France had thirty minutes to find a winning goal. But where would it come from? Before Alex knew it, it was the final minute of the match. Could France create one last chance? Gaël's panicky pass fell to an Irish defender instead, but he could only clear the ball to the edge of the penalty area.

Where Alex was waiting. This was it – his match-winning moment. His first touch was brilliant, but he

could see an Irish defender flying out towards him.
Oh well, he would just have to shoot straight away,
on the volley. He could do this.

Alex watched the ball carefully as it dropped onto
his bright red boot. *BANG!* Despite all the pressure,
it turned out to be one of his sweetest strikes ever. It
flew over the goalkeeper's outstretched arm and into
the top corner.

*Goooooooooooooooooooaaaaaaaaaaaaaaaallllllllllll
llllllllllllllll!!!!!!!!!!!!!!!!!!!!*

Now it was 2–1 – what a super sub! As he
watched the net bulge, Alex exploded with emotion.
He raced over to the sidelines, waggling his finger,
beating his chest, and screaming up at the stands, all
at the same time.

'Laca, you legend!' his teammates cheered when
they finally caught up with him. Alex was France's
hero and it was the greatest feeling of his young life.

So, had he made his manager change his mind?
Yes, for their second game against Spain, Smerecki
put Alex in the starting line-up ahead of Gilles.

'Well done, son!' his proud parents congratulated

him when he told them the good news on the phone. 'Now you've got to show the boss that you're there to stay.'

Sadly, however, it was his Lyon teammates who shone brightest. Yannis scored France's first goal, then Clément scored the second. And Alex? After sixty mostly frustrating minutes, Smerecki took him off.

'Well played,' his manager told him, but Alex knew that he was just being nice.

For the next match against Switzerland, he was back on the bench. Alex did come on in the second half, but by then, Yannis had already won the game with two more goals. His Lyon teammate was turning out to be the star of the tournament.

'So far,' Alex reminded himself. He still had two more games to be his team's hero again.

First up: a semi-final against the hosts, Turkey. At half-time, France were 1–0 down and in danger of going home in disappointment. Smerecki knew what to do – it was time to call on their super sub!

Alex made a difference straight away, and he

nearly scored with his first touch of the game. *So close!* He kept running and battling, until eventually France did get the ball in the net. *1–1!*

'Come on!' Alex was desperate to score the winning goal again, but in the end, he ran out of time. *Penalties!*

Right, so who was going to step up to the spot for France?

'Me!' said Yannis.

'Me!' said Gaël.

'Me!' said Gueïda Fofana.

'Me!' said Timothée Kolodziejczak.

And, of course: 'Me!' said Alex.

Alex's name was down to take the last one, and he was hoping that the shoot-out might be over by then. But no, Yannis missed, and after nine penalties, it was 3–3. The pressure was on! If he scored, Alex would win the game and send France into the final. If he missed... no, he didn't let that thought enter his head.

Looking as cool and calm as his hero Henry, Alex walked slowly forward, then ran up and... scored the winning spot-kick!

'Yes, yes, yes!' he shouted, punching the air. What an ice-cold penalty king! Alex wasn't celebrating alone for long; soon all of his teammates were jumping all over him.

Allez Les Bleus! Allez Les Bleus!

After a three-day rest, it was time for the big Under-17 Euro final when France would meet Spain for the second time! Their first match in the group stage had ended in an exciting 3–3 draw. So, who would win this time and lift the trophy?

'We will!' the French players cheered together as a team.

They knew that it was going to be another tough battle, though. Spain had lots of amazing attackers too, including Barcelona's Thiago Alcântara, who had scored two goals in their previous meeting with France.

'We need to start strongly,' Smerecki told the French squad before kick-off. 'Don't let them get their passing going.'

Despite scoring that winning spot-kick against

Turkey, Alex was back on the subs bench again. He couldn't help feeling disappointed, but hopefully he would get another chance to be France's super sub.

'Good luck, guys!' he told his friends Yannis and Clément. 'If we need a winning goal, I'll be waiting!'

Sadly, however, Alex's chance never came. Because after the strong start that their manager had asked for, France fell apart. Spain's attack was just too amazing.

1–0, 2–0, 3–0… 4–0!

'Oh no, this is getting embarrassing now!' Alex thought to himself, slumping in his seat. It was hard to watch his teammates struggling like that, especially as there was nothing he could do to help. Smerecki had made all three of his substitutions in the first fifty minutes, and none of them had involved Alex.

Oh well, never mind. 'We'll just have to win it next year instead!' Alex said by way of encouragement to his teammates.

Although France's Under-17 Euro adventure of 2008 had ended in defeat, Alex returned home with happy memories. He had scored a stunning volley against Ireland *and* the winning penalty against Turkey. Not bad for a first taste of international football!

CHAPTER 9

FIRING INTO THE FIRST TEAM

That summer, after Alex's international adventure, Lyon decided to offer senior contracts to two of their most talented young stars:

Yannis…

… and Clément.

'Well done, guys – you deserve it!'

Alex was pleased for his friends, but at the same time, he felt like the odd one out. After their happy years in the academy together as a trio, Yannis and Clément were now leaving him behind.

'Don't worry, you'll be joining us in no time!' they told him.

Alex was disappointed, but he wasn't worried.

No, he knew that he was good enough to become a professional player. He wasn't going to give up – no way. With lots of hard work and extra practice, he would surely follow Yannis and Clément and fire himself towards the Lyon first team.

'Great work, Alex – what a finish!' the youth coaches cheered. They were really impressed with his progress, and so was Sonny Anderson.

Lyon's star Brazilian striker had retired from football and was now coaching the club's attackers. He mostly worked with the first team squad, but every now and again he came to watch the academy training sessions as well.

'Wow, who's that?' Anderson asked, pointing to a youngster who had just smashed a shot into the top corner from thirty yards.

'Alexandre Lacazette,' the youth coach replied. 'Hopefully, he'll be moving up to work with you in the first team soon.'

'Great, I'll remember that name – that kid's going to be a top striker one day!'

But for now, Alex was ready to make the next

step-up from the Under-18s to the Lyon Reserves.
They played in the Championnat National 2, the
fourth division of French football. For the first time,
he would be playing against big, strong adults who
loved nothing more than battling against highly rated
youngsters like Alex.

'Welcome! My advice is, get some really good shin
pads,' Yannis joked – he was training with the first
team, while playing for the Reserves. 'Because trust
me, these defenders are going to kick you all game
long!'

At first, Alex found it really hard. In the academy,
he had been one of the most powerful players, but
now, he felt like a boy amongst big, angry men.

'Think you're a superstar, do you?' defenders
snarled at him, knocking him to the floor. 'Well, we'll
see about that!'

While Yannis banged in goal after goal, Alex went
game after game without scoring at all.

1, 2, 3, 4, 5, 6, 7, 8, 9...

What was going on? Alex wasn't playing that
badly, but he had lost his special shooting touch!

What had happened to the kid who Sonny Anderson said would be a top striker one day? What had happened to the boy who scored 122 goals in one season?

Alex was getting less game time every week – eighty minutes, then seventy, then fifty-five, then forty-five. If he didn't start scoring soon, Lyon's next young striker would come along and Alex would be moved to the subs bench in the Reserves. Meanwhile, Yannis and Clément were making their debuts for the first team…

'Relax, you'll find your form again,' Alex's brother Benoît told him. By now Benoît was playing as a defender for a club in Switzerland called Le Mont. 'Just keep working hard and believe!'

That's exactly what Alex did. He was so determined to succeed that he spent hours and hours practising his shooting on the football pitch after training.

He practised every possible finish, from every possible position, and from every possible angle.

GOAL! GOAL! GOAL!

Now Alex just needed to make the net bulge in a real Reserves match.

'Stay calm and stay confident,' the manager told him. 'That's when you're at your best.'

For the next game against Ajaccio, Alex started on the bench. But when Lyon went 2–0 up in the second half, it seemed like the perfect time for him to come on and score.

'Just go out there and enjoy yourself!' his manager shouted as he raced onto the pitch.

And Alex did just that. After only five minutes on the field, he got his first chance to shoot. 'Right, stay calm and stay confident,' he told himself. It was no big deal, no different to all those sweet strikes he had been hitting after training. *BANG!*

Gooooooooooooooooooooaaaaaaaaaaaaaaaaalllllllllllll llllllllllllllll!!!!!!!!!!!!!!!!!!!!

'Come on!' As he sprinted towards the corner flag to celebrate, Alex thought he might burst with joy and relief. At last, his scoreless streak was over! And before the final whistle blew, he even added a second. After going thirteen games without a goal, he now had two in less than thirty minutes.

'Well done, son!' Alfred shouted, dancing around as if he was the one who had scored the goals.

'Congratulations, kid – there'll be no stopping you now!' Alex's manager cheered, giving him a big hug.

With his shooting boots back on, Alex finished the 2008–09 season by scoring against Saint Priest, and Gap, and then also grabbing the winning goal against Fréjus St Raphaël.

Sonny Anderson had been right, after all! Five goals in six games – if Alex could keep up that top scoring form, he would fire his way into the Lyon first team in no time.

As soon as the new season started, Alex was scoring goals again.

One against Agde,

One against Bastia-Borgo,

One against Montpellier,

and then two against Toulon.

Wow, were the Lyon first-team coaches watching? Yes! And eventually, the manager, Claude Puel, called Alex up to come and train with the senior squad.

'Yes, yes, yes!' he cried out, punching the air. The hard work had all been worth it.

That first training session was a very exciting but nerve-wracking experience. As he entered the dressing room, Alex was surrounded by so many amazing international footballers: French goalkeeper Hugo Lloris, Croatian defender Dejan Lovren, Bosnian midfielder Miralem Pjanić, Brazilian winger Michel Bastos, Argentinian striker Lisandro López...

The list went on and on. Alex was a quiet guy anyway, but now he was star-struck too. Luckily, he could also see two more familiar faces: Yannis and Clément.

'Hey, look who's here!'

'Yes, Laca – the trio is back together at last!'

Once they got out on the training field, Alex tried his best to impress his new boss. He battled hard against Lyon's big defenders and he even dribbled through to score a goal against Lloris.

'Well done!' he heard the coaches cheer.

Alex was off to a strong start and, over the next few weeks, he settled into the squad nicely. His new teammates could see straight away that he had real star quality. So, when would he be ready for his huge next step: making his first team debut?

Lyon were fighting hard for the Ligue 1 title, so for now, their youngsters had to be patient. But in May 2010, just before his nineteenth birthday, Alex's big opportunity arrived at last. First, Puel put him on the bench for an away trip to Montpellier. That meant he had his own shirt number now – 38.

'Check me out!' Alex said to Clément, showing it off proudly.

He didn't get to come on in that match, but he did three days later, at home against Auxerre. With fifteen minutes to go, the score was still 1–1. Lyon had to win, otherwise the title race was over, and Marseille would be crowned champions.

Puel had already brought on one extra forward, but he decided that his team still needed more of an attacking threat.

'Alex, get ready,' one of the coaches called out to him. 'You're coming on!'

Before he had time to think, Alex was running

onto the field to make his debut for Lyon's first team. Wow, what an opportunity! Could he be a super sub and score the winning goal, like he had done for the France Under-17s?

'Yes, over here!'

As Lisandro crossed from the left, Alex sprinted in at the back post unmarked. The ball didn't reach him, though, because the Auxerre keeper punched it away, but only as far as Miralem. *GOAL – 2–1!*

The home crowd roared, and Alex was the first to high-five his brilliant teammate. He wasn't Lyon's hero this time, but one day very soon, he would be.

CHAPTER 10

FUTURE OF FRANCE PART 2

Just days after signing his first senior contract at Lyon, Alex joined up with the France squad for the 2010 Under-19 European Championships. He already knew most of his teammates from the Under-17s – Yannis, Clément, Gaël, Gilles – but there was one new player who he needed to meet. It was pretty hard to miss him with his spiky, blond hair.

'Hi, I'm Antoine,' he said. 'Antoine Griezmann.'

Alex was quiet, whereas Antoine was loud; Alex was a thinker, whereas Antoine was a joker. But despite their different characters, the two players formed a friendship straight away. It was like they had known each other for years. And fortunately for

France, they worked well together on the football pitch too.

'Great pass, Grizi!'

'Lovely finish, Laca!'

France were one of the favourites to win the whole tournament, especially now that they had Antoine in attack as well. And when the senior team were knocked out in the first round of the 2010 World Cup, there was even more pressure on the Under-19s to perform well. They even had the home crowd behind them, just like Alex's World Cup heroes back in 1998.

Allez Les Bleus! Allez Les Bleus!

But before Alex and co could even think about playing in another international final, they would have to get through the group stage.

Easy! France got off to a very strong start. They thrashed the Netherlands 4–1, although Alex was only on the pitch for the last twenty minutes. Next up: Austria. Antoine put France ahead in the first half, but they were struggling to score a second. So, Smerecki called on his super sub.

'Alex, you're coming on!'

'Thanks, Coach!' He was ready and raring to score. When the final whistle blew thirty-five minutes later, France had won 5–0 and Alex and Antoine had scored two goals each.

'We're just too hot to handle!' they joked as they celebrated together.

France were already through to the next round, so Smerecki left his deadly duo on the bench for the last group match against England.

'Save yourselves for the semi-finals,' he told them. 'We're going to need you against Croatia!'

France had lost in the semi-finals in both 2007 and 2009. This time, though, with the likes of Alex and Antoine in attack, surely they were good enough to go all the way?

But when Alex came on, it was still 1–1, with only twenty minutes to go. What could France's super sub do? As soon as the ball came to him, he sprinted away on the counterattack. Once he crossed the halfway line, Alex looked up and spotted Gaël in space, but a defender blocked the pass just in time.

So close! Still, his run had helped to get the French crowd going again.

Allez Les Bleus! Allez Les Bleus!

And Alex had got the French players going again too. A minute later, Francis Coquelin burst forward from midfield on a brilliant dribble and set up Cédric Bakambu to score. *2–1!*

'Come on!' Alex cheered as he raced across the pitch to join in the big squad celebrations.

France were through to another final, and they vowed that this time, they were going to win it. Alex and his teammates were determined to beat their old rivals, Spain, and lift that Under-19s Euro trophy.

'Remember that 4–0 thrashing two years ago?' Smerecki reminded everyone in his pre-game team talk.

The players nodded painfully. How could they ever forget an embarrassing defeat like that?

'Well, now is the time for revenge!'

For the first seventy minutes of the final, Alex sat anxiously on the bench, waiting for his manager's call. France had fought back bravely from 1–0 down, thanks to a goal from Gilles. But now, they needed some fresh legs and fresh ideas. Where was their super sub when they needed him?

'Alex, you're coming on!'

At last!

'Ready?' Smerecki asked him as they stood together on the sidelines.

'Ready!' Alex replied confidently. He was always prepared to help his team.

'Right, let's do this,' he said to himself as he ran on to replace Gilles. The Spanish defence was starting to look tired, and Alex was ready to run and run and run.

As soon as Gaël got the ball on the halfway line, *ZOOM!* Alex was off, sprinting towards the penalty area.

'Over here!' he screamed, but Gaël decided to go for goal himself.

Although the keeper saved his shot, Gaël was able to get to the rebound first.

'Over here!' Alex screamed again, this time waving his arms too. He was in so much space, if only his teammate would cross the ball…

Suddenly, it was floating through the air towards him, as if in slow motion. Alex watched it carefully, moving his body into the perfect heading position. He wouldn't get a better chance to score the winning goal for France.

As the ball dropped down, the Spanish defender on the line lifted up his boot, but Alex's head got there first.

Goooooooooooooooooooaaaaaaaaaaaaaaaaallllllllllll llllllllllllll!!!!!!!!!!!!!!!!!!!!

'Yes, yes, yes!' Alex cried out, with his dreadlocks flying everywhere. As he ran towards the bench, he blew kisses to all the friends and family – and to the French supporters – in the stadium. It was the new greatest feeling of his young life.

While the Spanish players sank to their knees in despair, the French players jumped on their hero with joy.

'Yes, Laca – I just knew you'd get the winner!'

'Hey, even I couldn't have scored that one, super sub!'

'Come on, concentrate – only five minutes left!'

They were the longest five minutes of Alex's life, but France held on for the victory. At the final whistle, he leapt high into the air and then ran around hugging all of his teammates. It was party time – thanks to Alex's header, they were the new Under-19 European Champions!

Allez Les Bleus! Allez Les Bleus!

Campeones, Campeones, Olé! Olé! Olé!

Alex had won his first international trophy, and hopefully, it wouldn't be his last.

CHAPTER 11

THE BIG BREAKTHROUGH

Alex deserved a holiday after his Under-19s Euro adventure, but he didn't get one. Instead, the day after his winning goal for France, he was back playing for Lyon, this time in London in their preseason Emirates Cup game against Celtic.

And not only did Alex play, but he also set up his team's second goal. It was a classic Lyon academy move. After running onto Clément's clever through ball, Alex cut it back to Harry Novillo in the middle.

'Now that's teamwork!' The three youngsters celebrated together.

Alex didn't last the full ninety minutes, but that was only because Puel took him off.

'Mate, you must be exhausted,' his teammate

Michel Bastos said, marvelling at his stamina, 'and we've got another game against AC Milan tomorrow!'

Yes, Alex was tired after staying up late celebrating and then catching an early morning train, but he was also determined to break into the Lyon starting XI as soon as possible. And if that meant playing three matches in three days, then he didn't mind at all.

'Don't worry, I'll have plenty of time to rest when I retire!' he promised his mum.

Alex started the new season playing for the Lyon Reserves again, but he didn't stay there for long. By the end of September, he was back on the first team bench, and by the end of October, he was even getting some game-time.

'Alex, you're coming on!'

Although he didn't quite manage to score the winning goal against AC Arles, Alex could feel himself improving with every minute of every match. It was surely only a matter of time before he scored his first senior goal for Lyon.

In the next Ligue 1 match against FC Sochaux,

Lyon were winning 1–0 late in the first half when Michel Bastos got an injury. He would have to come off, but who would come on? Puel looked at his subs bench and picked Alex to play on the right wing. Brilliant – he had over forty-five minutes to make his mark!

But before Alex could do anything, Sochaux scored to make it 1–1. Oh well, Lyon were going to need a winning goal now...

Just minutes after the equaliser, Alex got the ball just inside the Sochaux box. 'Here we go!' he thought to himself. 'My time to shine!'

As his marker backed away, Alex shifted it to the right and fired a shot at goal. The keeper saved it, but the defender's clearance fell at Alex's feet again. Phew, another chance! He faked to shoot with his left, but then dragged it on to his right instead. With a bit of help from a deflection, Alex's second strike flew over the keeper and into the roof of the net.

Goooooooooooooooooooooaaaaaaaaaaaaaaaalllllllllllll llllllllllllllll!!!!!!!!!!!!!!!!!!!!

Hopefully, he would go on to score better goals

than that in the future, but for now, Alex was off the mark, Lyon were winning, and that was all that mattered.

'Nice one, Laca!' Clément cheered as they celebrated together.

Three days later, Alex was called into action again. In the Champions League, Lyon were losing 4–0 away at Portuguese club Benfica.

'Just go out there and see what you can do,' Puel said, taking the pressure off his young forward.

'Sure thing, Coach!'

Alex loved playing with freedom; that way, he could use his natural flair. As soon as he got the ball, he pushed forward on the attack. After dribbling down the right wing, he crossed it to Yoann Gourcuff near the penalty spot. *4–1!*

The fightback was on! Ten minutes later, Alex flicked on Yoann's corner and Bafétimbi Gomis tapped in at the back post. *4–2!*

'Thanks, Laca!' Bafétimbi cheered, giving him a quick high-five as they ran back for the restart.

'Come on!' Alex called out, waving his arms

up and down to try to motivate his teammates. Although he preferred to stay quiet, he wasn't afraid to speak up when he needed to. It was probably too late for Lyon to win the game, but maybe they could get the most unlikely of draws? Stranger things had happened in football...

Dejan did score a header to make it 4–3, but by then, unfortunately, it was the last minute of the game. They had been so close to making an incredible comeback! At the final whistle, the club's supporters were cheering, not booing – because although Lyon had lost the game, they had found a new hero.

'What a performance!' Puel cried out, giving his young star a great big hug.

'Thanks, Boss, and thanks for believing in me,' Alex replied.

First the winning goal in the Under-19 Euro final, and now two assists on his Champions League debut – at the age of nineteen, Alex was already building a reputation as a real big game player.

After the match, everyone was talking about

Lyon's next superstar. Was he going to be the next Karim Benzema? Or the next Loïc Rémy? Or even the next Thierry Henry? No, Alex was just Alex, but he had officially made his big breakthrough.

A month later, Alex made it doubly sure that he was one to watch. Lyon were losing 2–1 to Hapoel Tel Aviv when he entered the game. He had work to do because his team needed at least one point to make it through to the Champions League Round of 16.

'I've got this,' Alex told himself, taking a moment to focus his mind on scoring.

As the final whistle drew closer and closer, Lisandro dribbled in off the left wing, looking for a forward pass to play.

'Yes, over here!' Alex called out, bursting into the gap between the Hapoel centre-backs.

When the pass arrived, he kept his cool. He dribbled past one last diving defender and then smashed a shot into the bottom corner. 2–2!

Goooooooooooooooooooooaaaaaaaaaaaaaaaaalllllllllllll llllllllllllll!!!!!!!!!!!!!!!!!

'Yeeeeeesss!' he screamed, throwing his arms out wide as his teammates rushed over to congratulate him.

Alex had his first Champions League goal, to go with those two assists against Benfica. At this rate, it wouldn't be very long before Lyon's young super sub would break into the starting XI.

CHAPTER 12

FUTURE OF FRANCE PART 3

France's prize for winning the Under-19 Euros was a place at the 2011 Under-20 World Cup. Alex couldn't wait to travel all the way to Colombia with his friends – Clément, Yannis, Gaël, Gilles, Francis and, of course, Antoine. Hopefully, it was going to be the trip – and tournament – of a lifetime.

Les Bleus had never won the Under-20 World Cup before, or even made it through to the semi-finals. So Alex and co had a real chance of making history for France, as well as making a name for themselves in front of all the watching scouts. So many superstars had started their careers by winning this tournament: Diego Maradona in 1979, Xavi in 1999, Dani Alves in

2003, Lionel Messi in 2005, Sergio Agüero in 2007...

So, who would win the Best Player award in 2011? After his big breakthrough season at Lyon, Alex was feeling calm and confident. After all, his international record so far was really, really good: 2008 – one winning goal and one winning penalty at the Under-17s Euros, and 2010 – three goals, including the tournament winner, at the Under-19 Euros.

Alex believed in himself. Alongside Antoine and his other teammates, he was a big part of the future of French football.

Once in Colombia, that future didn't look so bright, however, when France were thrashed 4–1 by the hosts in the first match of the tournament. Alex came on for Cédric at half-time, with the score still at 1–1. But he could only watch in shock as James Rodríguez and Luis Muriel ran through the France defence again and again.

What a disaster! It was the worst possible start for the European Champions. After the match, there was a deathly silence in the dressing room.

'That's your wake-up call,' Smerecki warned his

players angrily. 'Don't you ever walk out onto that pitch again and just expect to beat your opponents! You have to earn your wins – every single one of them. That means defending as a team *and* taking your chances in attack.'

Alex looked guiltily down at the dressing room floor. He had missed a golden chance, back when they were only 2–1 down. If he had scored, things could have been so different... Oh well, he would just have to make up for his mistake in the next match against South Korea. France had to win, otherwise they would be heading home already.

When Alex came on against South Korea, once again the game was tied at 1–1. But this time, he helped fire his team to victory. Gueïda scored France's second goal and then Alex made sure with the third. *3–1!*

Now, if they could just beat Mali, France's World Cup would be back on track. Once more, France were saved by their determined super sub. It was still 0–0 when Alex came on for Antoine, but the score didn't stay that way for long.

Alex played a great one-two with Clément and then slipped a clever pass across to Cédric. *1–0!*

Alex ran onto Clément's through ball and scored from what looked like an impossible angle. *2–0!*

Goooooooooooooooooooaaaaaaaaaaaaaaaaalllllllllllll lllllllllllll!!!!!!!!!!!!!!!!!!!!

As he raced off to celebrate, Alex blew a cheeky kiss at the TV camera. One goal and one assist – yes, he was really making a name for himself now.

The France players walked around the pitch, clapping the supporters. Despite their earlier awful defeat to Colombia, they were through to the second round.

'Laca, what would we do without you?' Francis asked.

Alex's answer was short, simple and true: 'Lose!'

In the Round of 16 against Ecuador, it was Antoine's turn to be France's hero. But then in the quarter-final against Nigeria, it was Alex to the rescue again.

This time, he came on in the first half, giving him even more time to grab that winning goal. Alex thought it was mission complete early in the second half, when he collected Clément's pass and fired the ball past the keeper. When he was in that kind of scoring form, he never missed.

Goooooooooooooooooooooaaaaaaaaaaaaaaaaaallllllllllllll llllllllllllllll!!!!!!!!!!!!!!!!!!!

1–0! Alex hurdled the advertising boards and danced happily with Cédric in front of the fans. It felt so good to be France's hero once more. But just when they were starting to think about the semi-finals, Nigeria scored a very late equaliser.

'Noooooo!' the French defenders groaned, but Alex just shrugged and got on with the game. Oh well, he would just have to score another winner in extra time…

Gueïda made it 2–1 with a stunning strike, but Alex knew that the match still wasn't over yet. Not while France were only winning by one goal. So when Gaël raced away down the right wing, Alex did the same on the left.

'Yes, over here!' he called out for the ball.

Alex was in so much space on the edge of the

penalty area. When the pass arrived, he calmly dribbled around the keeper and then shot past two defenders on the line.

Gooooooooooooooooooaaaaaaaaaaaaaaaaalllllllllllllll lllllllllllllll!!!!!!!!!!!!!!!!!!!!

The score was 3–1 – now it really was game over! Alex gave Gaël a big hug to say thanks for the assist, and then punched the air with passion. France were through to the Under-20 World Cup semi-finals for the first time, and he was having his best international tournament ever!

Unfortunately, France couldn't make it past Portugal in the semi-finals, but there was still time for Alex to add one more goal to his total. Early on in the third-place play-off against Mexico, Timothée Kolodziejczak delivered a teasing cross from the left. Alex was the only attacker in the box, with three defenders around him, but he leapt up highest and headed the ball powerfully past the keeper.

Gooooooooooooooooooaaaaaaaaaaaaaaaaalllllllllllllll lllllllllllllll!!!!!!!!!!!!!!!!!!!!

Another game, another goal – Alex was on fire!

Although Mexico fought back to win the game, he left Colombia feeling proud of his performances. He had certainly proved that he was a big part of the future of French football.

In the end, Brazil's striker Henrique won the Best Player award, but Alex finished as the tournament's joint top scorer with five goals. Not a bad result for a super sub!

CHAPTER 13

UPS AND DOWNS

The 2011–12 season was all set to be a brilliant one for Alex. After his goals at the Under-20 World Cup, he was France's top young forward now. And having started out wearing the Number 38 shirt at Lyon, he was now Number 17, a clear sign that his club believed in him. Hopefully, he would get lots of game-time in Ligue 1, the two French cups *and* the Champions League.

'You, Lisandro, Michel Bastos and Gomis – what a top-quality attack!' Alfred told his son excitedly.

With that awesome line-up, Lyon were aiming to win the French league again. It was now three years since the last of their seven titles in a row.

'Come on, we need to get back to the glory days!'

the club's supporters urged.

Like always, Alex just wanted to play as much football as possible for Lyon. If his club's new manager, Rémi Garde, asked him to attack down the left, then that's what he would do. In fact, even if Garde had asked him to go in goal, he would have said yes, just as long as his mum let him!

The problem was that without a fixed position, Alex was finding it hard to settle into the Lyon first team. Sometimes he was on the left, sometimes he was on the right, sometimes he was in the middle, and sometimes he was on the bench. One thing was for sure, though – Alex wasn't playing to his full potential. Just a single goal in his first fourteen games was nowhere near good enough for France's top young forward.

'Don't worry, you're still learning at this level,' Garde reassured him. 'You'll find your best form again soon. Until then, just keep working hard for the team. We need you!'

After a slow start, the old Alex gradually returned. He still wasn't as consistent as he wanted to be, but at least he was producing moments of magic again. He scored the winner away at FC Lorient, and then set up the opening goal for Jimmy Briand against Thonon Évian.

'That's more like it!' Alex thought to himself.

As 2012 began, he felt he was back at his best, just in time for Lyon's busiest part of the season. They were still in all four competitions, but could they go all the way and lift a trophy or two? Alex was up for the challenge.

In the Coupe de la Ligue semi-final, Lyon were losing 2–0 to Lorient when Alex led the amazing fightback. He collected Kim Källström's pass, shifted the ball onto his right foot and *BANG!* Even though he was outside the penalty area and falling off balance, he still made the strike look so easy.

Goooooooooooooooooooaaaaaaaaaaaaaaaalllllllllllll lllllllllllll!!!!!!!!!!!!!!!!!

'Let's go – there's still ten minutes left!' Alex shouted loudly as they ran back for the restart.

Suddenly, the Lyon players were all pumped up. Jimmy headed home a very late equaliser and then in extra time, Bafétimbi and Alex scored one each to send Lyon into the final.

'Great work, Laca!' Michel Bastos cheered as they celebrated together on the pitch. 'We won that game thanks to you.'

Alex was always happy to help his team, especially when there was a trophy to aim for. Next up was APOEL Nicosia in the Champions League Last 16. The first leg was at home at the Stade de Gerland, so Lyon were desperate to win. They needed a hero, but who? Alex, of course! Picking the ball up on the left side of the area, he cut inside beautifully and hit a powerful shot that looped up over the keeper. 1–0!

Goooooooooooooooooooaaaaaaaaaaaaaaaaalllllllllllll llllllllllllll!!!!!!!!!!!!!!!!!!!

It was another Champions League cracker! This time, Alex didn't say anything because he didn't need to – his brilliant right foot had done the talking for him. As his teammates hugged him by the corner flag, he could hear thousands of fans chanting his name:

Alexandre Lacazette, Lacazette, Lacazette!

Alexandre Lacazette, woah oah!

It was an amazing feeling, but sadly, by March, Lyon were out of the Champions League and out of the Ligue 1 title race too. Never mind, though – at least they still had two trophies left to fight for.

In the Coupe de France, Alex led his team all the way to the final, with a goal against Bordeaux in the Round of 16 and then another against Ajaccio in the semis.

Lyon now had two cup finals in two weeks – could they win them both? Alex was up for the challenge.

First, they faced Marseille in the Coupe de la Ligue. The atmosphere was electric at the Stade de France in Paris, with the noise of nearly 80,000 passionate supporters. Alex had a long time to listen because he was sat on the bench until the 106th minute. Boring! But wait...

'Get ready – you're coming on!'

Marseille had just scored in extra time, so Lyon were sending on their super sub to try and save the day. Could Alex do what he had done for the France youth teams so many times before?

Unfortunately, there just wasn't enough time. Before he could really get into the game, it was all over and Lyon had lost. Alex walked around the pitch, shaking hands like a good sport, but inside he was feeling so frustrated.

Why hadn't Garde picked him to play from the start? Or at least brought him on in the second half?

'Hey, heads up,' Bafétimbi said, putting an arm around his slumped shoulders. 'Remember, we're back here in two weeks. We've got another chance to win a cup final this season!'

A fortnight later, in the Coupe de France against Quevilly-Rouen, Alex started in attack alongside Bafétimbi and Lisandro. Much better!

Lyon were the favourites to win the final, but that made things even more difficult. With Quevilly-Rouen defending deep on the edge of their box, it was hard to find a way through. It was going to take a moment of magic, something special, something like a terrific team move...

Just as the Lyon fans began to grow restless,

Clément played a quick one-two with Alex, then passed it forward to Bafétimbi, who flicked it through to Alex.

'That's it!' the supporters cheered, rising out of their seats.

At last, Alex was into the area! He dribbled around the Quevilly-Rouen keeper, but the angle was now too tight for a shot. So, with his left foot, he chipped a cross towards the penalty spot, where Lisandro was waiting to volley it in. *1–0!*

Lisandro was Lyon's goalscoring hero, but he didn't forget about his assistant. He raced over to Alex and they celebrated together, in front of their joyful fans.

'Come on, that trophy is *ours!*'

They had to wait another sixty-five minutes, but eventually the cup did belong to Lyon. What a feeling! It had been a season of ups and downs for Alex. Ten goals in forty-three games wasn't a record that he was particularly pleased with, but at least he was ending the year on a high, with a winner's medal and a big, shiny trophy.

On the stage, the countdown began: 3, 2, 1…

'Hurraaaaay!' Alex cheered with everyone else, throwing his arms up in the air.

CHAPTER 14

LISTENING TO A LEGEND

With his first full club season at Lyon behind him,
Alex took a well-deserved holiday. Ah, relaxation! It
was nice to just hang out with his parents and have
a laugh with his brothers, without having to worry
about his next match. He needed a break because
he had been playing non-stop football since the
Under-20 World Cup the previous summer.

But Alex's mind was soon moving on to bigger
and better things. In the 2012–13 season, he wanted
more – for himself and for his team. More goals,
more assists and, best of all, more trophies.

The new season started well, as Lyon beat
Montpellier on penalties to lift the Champions'
Trophy. Although Alex didn't take one of the

spot-kicks, he did set up Jimmy's late equaliser with a brilliant cross to the back post.

'Thanks, Laca!' his strike partner cheered.

A few minutes later, Jimmy tried to repay the favour by passing the ball across to Alex. He was only eight yards out, with pretty much an open goal in front of him. The Lyon fans were already on their feet, thinking it was a certain winner. But somehow, Alex scuffed his shot wide.

'Noooooo!' he groaned, swatting the air angrily. 'How did I miss that?'

Although Lyon did still win that match, missing shots became the story of Alex's season. He was playing well and creating lots of chances for his teammates, but he wasn't scoring enough goals himself. By Christmas, he only had two across all competitions; by the end of the campaign, he had four.

'Four!' Alex repeated, shaking his head in disbelief. 'Even Clément scored seven and he plays in midfield!'

'Okay, but don't forget about your ten assists,'

Alfred replied, trying to make his son feel better.

That was true, and Alex was also playing as a winger rather than a proper striker, but still – he was a whole lot better than four goals in thirty-seven games, wasn't he? His scoring record was supposed to be improving, not getting worse!

Although things weren't going as well as Alex had hoped, he was still living his childhood dream of being a Lyon player. He couldn't forget how fortunate he was to be doing what he loved every day – playing football, and earning lots of money for it.

'Maybe I should just be satisfied with what I've achieved so far,' Alex began to think. 'I *am* only twenty-two, after all!'

But then a chance meeting with his greatest football hero changed everything. In July 2013, Lyon travelled to the USA on a preseason tour, and who was the New York Red Bulls' star striker? Thierry Henry!

Henry didn't play in the 2–2 draw, but he was there watching. After the game, he came over to speak to Alex.

'It's nice to meet you – I've heard good things about you!'

At first, Alex stood there in a star-struck daze, thinking, 'Wow, am I actually talking to Thierry Henry?' But he soon calmed down and started to listen, because the Arsenal legend had lots of interesting advice to give him.

'Look, the hard work never stops, okay?' Henry told him. 'If you want to be the best, you've got to keep testing yourself. You can't get comfortable, and right now, you seem too comfortable to me. I remember when I was your age and I got my big move to Juventus. At first, I thought I could just relax and enjoy myself, now that I had made it to the big time. But I was wrong – you can't ever think like that! Not if you want to reach the top, anyway – and you do want to reach the top, don't you?'

Alex nodded eagerly. Of course he did!

'Good, then you've got to keep working on yourself and find your perfect position. Anyone can see you've got lots of potential, but now you've got to make the most of it. What kind of an attacker do you really want to be – a winger, a Number 10, a striker?'

'A striker – like you.'

Henry laughed. 'Correct answer! Well, then you've got to set yourself targets. How many goals did you score last season?'

Alex looked down at the floor in embarrassment. It was hard to admit but there was no point in lying.

'Four.'

'Okay, well you can definitely improve on that! So, come on – how many goals are you going to score this season?'

Hmm, Alex had to think about that one. He didn't want to aim too high, but he didn't want to aim too low either. What seemed achievable?

'Fifteen?' he suggested eventually.

Henry nodded. 'Yeah, that seems like a good place to start, but remember, that's only the start, okay? Once you've reached fifteen, you then aim higher – twenty, then twenty-five, then thirty!'

Alex smiled. The idea of scoring thirty goals seemed like a far-away dream at that moment, but one day maybe. If he wanted to be a superstar striker, then confidence was key.

'Thanks for all the advice,' he told Henry as they said their goodbyes. 'I think that was the wake-up call I needed.'

'My pleasure – I just don't want to see you waste all that talent.'

'I won't!' Alex promised.

After talking to his hero, Alex was ready to aim higher again. He knew it was time for him to light up Ligue 1, with goals as well as assists.

CHAPTER 15

LIGHTING UP LIGUE 1

As Clément played the pass, Alex took a few steps to the left, away from his marker. It was a classic striker's move, and that's what he was now – a striker, Lyon's lethal Number 10.

When the Nice centre-back missed his header, Alex pounced. He took one touch to control it, another to dribble into the penalty area, and then he calmly placed his shot past the keeper.

Gooooooooooooooooooooaaaaaaaaaaaaaaaaalllllllllllll llllllllllllll!!!!!!!!!!!!!!!!!!!

It was only the thirteenth minute on the opening day of the new season, and Alex was already off the mark. But there was no big celebration: no – he just threw his arms out wide and nodded his head as if he scored all the time.

After his talk with Thierry Henry, Alex was a stone-cold striker these days. In the second half of the game, he started his run in his own half, as he chased after Yoann's through ball. The Nice keeper rushed out to stop him, but Alex just dribbled around him and passed it into the empty net. *3–0!*

What a start! Six days later, he scored again, away at Sochaux. Now, the only thing stopping Alex was his discipline. He was so determined to win that he got himself sent off twice in just three league matches. Both times, Alex was already on a yellow card, but he still kept flying into tackles.

'Not again!' he groaned as he trudged off the pitch. Why did he keep letting Lyon down?

'Hey, you just need to calm down and think about what you're doing,' Lyon's manager Rémi Garde told Alex as he sat despairing in the dressing room. 'I know you're trying to help the team, but you can't help us if you're suspended all the time!'

At the end of the game, Alex apologised to his teammates. 'Sorry guys, it won't happen again. From now on, I'm all about goals.'

On his return from suspension, it only took twelve minutes for Alex to score against Guingamp. He used his strength to hold off the defender and then fired the ball into the bottom corner.

'I'm back!' he told Clément with a cheeky smile.

That was brilliant news, because Lyon's next game was against their big local rivals, Saint-Étienne.

It was never easy playing away at the Stade Geoffroy-Guichard, surrounded by green on all sides, but Alex was desperate to make up for his mistakes. If he could just be Lyon's 'Le Derby' hero, all would be forgiven.

Early in the second half, Bafétimbi jumped and sent a powerful header goalwards. The Lyon supporters in the stadium held their breath. Was this going to be the opening goal?

Although Alex was hoping that his strike partner would score, he raced in for the rebound just in case. That turned out to be a very wise decision because the Saint-Étienne keeper couldn't hold on to the ball. It squirmed out towards Alex, who got there ahead of the defenders and blasted it joyfully into the roof of the net.

Goooooooooooooooooooaaaaaaaaaaaaaaaaalllllllllllll lllllllllllll!!!!!!!!!!!!!!!!!!!!

Yes, scoring in 'Le Derby' made everything much better, and so did cheekily shushing the Saint-Étienne supporters behind the goal! The Lyon fans loved it, and they chanted his name as loudly as they could:

Alexandre Lacazette, Lacazette, Lacazette!
Alexandre Lacazette, woah oah!

At the final whistle, the Lyon players celebrated as if they'd just won the league. That's what winning 'Le Derby' meant to them.

With another double against Thonon Évian, Alex was up to twelve league goals by February. And that wasn't even including the cup competitions. With two goals in the Coupe de France and one in the Coupe de la Ligue, that made a total of… fifteen. Hurray, Alex had reached his target already!

But what was it that Thierry Henry had said to him? 'Once you've reached fifteen, you then aim higher – twenty, then twenty-five, then thirty!'

So, Alex upped his target to twenty. That seemed easily achievable, with four months of the season still to go.

It wasn't just about the goals, though; Alex was important to Lyon in lots of ways. With his strength and skill, he could hold the ball up and create chances for Bafétimbi, Jimmy and Clément.

Whenever Alex was on the pitch, the Lyon fans never gave up hope. There was always a chance of something special happening. In the Coupe de la Ligue in particular, Alex was simply unstoppable. He scored against Reims, he scored against Troyes, and he set up Bafétimbi's winner against Marseille too.

What a hero! Thanks to Alex, Lyon were through to the final again, their third in three years. This time, however, they were up against the French league champions, PSG.

It was going to be a very tough test, especially for Alex. He was going head-to-head with one of the best strikeforces in the world. PSG's top scorer, Zlatan Ibrahimović, was out injured, but that still left Lucas Moura and Edinson Cavani.

Oh well, thought Alex, what was it that Henry had said to him? 'If you want to be the best, you've got to keep testing yourself.'

A lot had changed since Alex's last trip to the Stade de France, for the same final two years earlier – his shirt number, his position and, most importantly of all, his confidence.

Alex had already reached his second goal target of the season – twenty. He was Lyon's top scorer and their number one danger man. The Coupe de la Ligue final was just another opportunity to show his quality, in front of nearly 80,000 fans, plus the millions more watching at home on TV.

'Come on, let's do this!' Alex cheered as the teams waited in the tunnel.

Unfortunately, Lyon got off to the worst possible start. In only the fourth minute of the match, Cavani scored from a goalmouth scramble.

'Keep going!' Garde encouraged his players. 'There's plenty of time left!'

Bafétimbi nearly equalised with a header, but then PSG went straight down the other end and won a penalty. *2–0!*

Uh oh, Lyon were in real trouble now! The
supporters looked to their star man – what could
Alex do to save the day?

Early in the second half, Alex got the ball just
inside the PSG half. He could see Bafétimbi ahead
of him, but he was busy running to the left, and was
creating space for Alex to dribble into.

'Sure, why not?' Alex thought to himself. He had
to at least try.

With a burst of pure pace, Alex raced forward on
the attack. Two PSG defenders tried to chase him,
but they couldn't keep up.

'Shoot!' the fans urged.

Alex was still outside the penalty area, but he
could see more defenders closing in. It was now or
never. With a swing of his right leg, he sent the ball
skidding into the bottom corner.

*Gooooooooooooooooooooaaaaaaaaaaaaaaaaalllllllllllll
lllllllllllllll!!!!!!!!!!!!!!!!!!!*

Alex had scored an absolute wonderstrike, and
another big game goal. But there was no time to

celebrate because Lyon were back in the game! He grabbed the ball out of the net and carried it all the way to the halfway line. Now, they just needed one more goal…

But as hard as they tried, Lyon couldn't score a second. At the final whistle, Alex stared down at the grass in disappointment.

'Unlucky,' Cavani said, coming over to shake his hand. 'Well played today.'

Losing in a final was always hard to take, but at least Lyon had managed to fight back to 2–1. They could be proud of their performance, and especially of Alex, their shining star.

'I hope Henry was watching my wondergoal!' he thought to himself.

CHAPTER 16

A GOOD FIT FOR FRANCE?

Didier Deschamps was definitely one who had been watching Alex's wondergoal in the cup final. In fact, France's national team manager had been keeping a close eye on him for years. France already had a strong, settled squad with the 2014 World Cup coming up that summer, but there was always room for a bright new star...

Alex had been called up to the senior squad for the first time back in June 2013. France had been playing friendlies against Uruguay and Brazil, and their winger Jérémy Ménez had pulled out with a last-minute injury.

'Thanks, that's the best news ever!' Alex told Deschamps when he got the call.

After progressing through the national youth teams – from the Under-16s all the way up to the Under-21s – Alex had always dreamed that this day would come.

'Mum, Dad, I'm going to be a senior international!' he cheered happily. His childhood dream was about to come true.

It was a long flight to South America, but Alex didn't mind at all. He had a huge match to prepare for and plus, he had Clément, Bafétimbi, Hugo and Yoann there to entertain him.

'It's just like being back at Lyon!' he joked, pushing his seat back to try to get some sleep.

This was Alex's first time in the France squad, so he wasn't expecting to be in the Starting XI. Still, he tried his best to impress Deschamps in the team training sessions. Hopefully he would at least get to come on and make his debut at some point.

By half-time, Alex was growing very restless on the bench. It was 0–0, and a very boring 0–0 at that. What the game needed was a spark, a bit of excitement…

Sadly, that kind of excitement didn't arrive in the form of Alex; it arrived in the form of a Luis Suárez goal. It was 1–0 to Uruguay!

Ten minutes later, Deschamps finally decided to make his first changes. First, Bafétimbi came on for Olivier Giroud, and then Alex came on for Yoann.

'Good luck!' his Lyon teammate said as they high-fived on the touchline.

'Thanks!'

Wearing Number 14 on the back of his blue shirt, Alex was officially a senior French international now. Right, he had half an hour to make an impact. It was time to be his country's super sub yet again.

But as the minutes ticked by, Alex hardly touched the ball. It was a terrible game and sadly there was nothing he could do to make it better.

As he shook hands with the Uruguay players at the final whistle, Alex felt very unsatisfied. What if that was his only chance? What if Deschamps dropped him for the Brazil game?

But he didn't. Against Brazil, with twenty-five minutes to go, France were losing 1–0 again, so their manager made a triple attacking substitution, bringing on Olivier, Clément *and* Alex! But as they pushed forward looking for an equaliser, Brazil punished them on the counterattack.

2–0!

3–0!

What a disaster! By the time the final whistle went, Alex was wondering if he should have just said no to Deschamps and stayed at home instead.

'There's no way I'm going to the World Cup now!' he moaned to his brothers when he got back to Lyon.

But since his disappointing France debut, a lot had changed for Alex. He had met his hero Thierry Henry, who had inspired him to keep working hard and improving his game. Now, after lighting up Ligue 1 during the 2013–14 season, Alex might just have a chance of making Deschamps's squad for the World Cup in Brazil – and his boss at Lyon felt the same way.

'The manager is aware of the huge improvement made by Alex since the start of the season,' Garde told the media. 'He knows he can score important goals.'

So, on the day of the big announcement, Alex waited anxiously for his phone to ring. Had he done enough to impress Deschamps? France could only take twenty-three players to the tournament, and there were so many other amazing attackers to choose from: creative playmakers like his friend Clément, and Rémy Cabella and Samir Nasri, tricky wingers like his friend Antoine, and Mathieu Valbuena and Franck Ribéry, and goalscoring strikers like Karim Benzema, Olivier Giroud and Loïc Rémy.

There was no way that they would all be going to Brazil! No, the France manager had some very difficult decisions to make.

'I'm so sorry, Alex,' Deschamps told him on the phone, 'but for a World Cup, I have to pick what I think is the best squad, not just the best twenty-three players. I hope you understand.'

Alex did understand, but that didn't make him feel any less disappointed. Clément and Antoine would both be going to Brazil, leaving him behind to watch the tournament on TV.

'It's going to be such a boring summer now!' he moaned to himself. 'Why did I get my hopes up like that?'

Alex's World Cup dream wasn't over yet, though. He was one of seven players on France's standby list. So, if any of their attackers got injured before the tournament started, he might still be on that flight to Brazil.

'You never know what might happen,' Rose said, trying to lift her son's spirits. 'Don't go booking a holiday just yet!'

As it turned out, in the days leading up to France's first match against Honduras, two attackers had to pull out of the squad with injury: Franck and Clément. Alex was gutted for his good friend Clément, but was his own World Cup wish about to come true?

That was too much to hope for. No – Deschamps decided to replace Clément with midfielder Morgan Schneiderlin, and to replace Franck with Rémy.

Nooooo! Oh well, Alex's World Cup dream would just have to wait for another four years. In the meantime, a holiday in the sun would be the perfect preparation for another season of hard work on the football pitch.

CHAPTER 17

2014–15: A TOP-SCORING SEASON

By the time the new Ligue 1 season started, Bafétimbi and Jimmy had both left Lyon. Alex was sad to see them go; now, he really was the star striker. His local club was relying on him more than ever. The pressure was on to score plenty of goals.

Pressure? What pressure? Alex was on fire, right from game one.

He scored from the spot against Stade Rennais. *GOAL!*

He guided the ball into the bottom corner against Toulouse. *GOAL!*

He tapped in at the back post against Metz. *GOAL!*

He scored from outside the box against Lorient.

GOAL!

Any distance, any angle: Alex always knew how to
find the back of the net. He was Lyon's leading scorer
now, full of calm and confidence.

So, what next? Alex wanted more. He could hear
his hero Thierry Henry in his head, telling him to
keep raising his target. What hadn't he done yet?
Ah yes, of course – score a professional hat-trick!
He hadn't scored three goals in a game since his
academy days with Yannis and Clément. Nothing
said 'star striker' like an amazing hat-trick.

By half-time in Lyon's home match against Lille,
Alex was only one goal away. 'This is my moment,'
he told himself.

To score his first goal, Alex had shown off all
his best qualities: speed to chase after Nabil Fekir's
through ball, strength to outmuscle the last defender,
and then shooting to beat the keeper.

*Goooooooooooooooooooooaaaaaaaaaaaaaaaaalllllllllllll
llllllllllllll!!!!!!!!!!!!!!!!!!!*

Alex's second had been a powerful header from a
Yoann free kick. So, what about the third? He didn't

really care, just so long as he completed his hat-trick.

'Yes, over here!' Alex called out to his teammate, Clinton N'Jie. With time running out, he had raced forward at full speed, all the way from one box to the other. Although his legs were tired, he was desperate to score a third.

When the pass arrived, Alex dribbled into the penalty area and then paused for a split second to think. What was the best way to score? Because he wasn't going to waste this golden chance – no way!

As Alex paused, two Lille players dived in front of him. A-ha, he knew what to do now! With a drop of the shoulder, he dribbled around one defender and then fired the ball past the other and into the bottom corner. He made it look so easy, like he had all the time in the world.

Gooooooooooooooooooooaaaaaaaaaaaaaaaaalllllllllllll llllllllllllll!!!!!!!!!!!!!!!!!!

Alex was now officially a hat-trick hero, and what a way to do it! 'Follow me!' he shouted excitedly, calling Clinton and his other teammates over to the corner flag to celebrate with him in front of the fans.

Alexandre Lacazette, Lacazette, Lacazette!
Alexandre Lacazette, woah oah!

It was another special moment that Alex would never forget.

'Did you see that, Deschamps?' he thought to himself. He really hoped that the France manager was still watching him because he was now better than ever.

So, what next? Alex had scored seven goals in his first nine games, which was more than Zlatan and more than Cavani too. Could he keep firing and finish the season as the Ligue 1 top scorer? That was his ambitious new target. If Alex wanted to become a world-class striker, then consistency was key. Challenge accepted!

He scored a swerving long-range rocket against Montpellier. *GOAL!*

Wearing the Lyon captain's armband with pride, he added two more screamers against Nice. *GOAL! GOAL!*

Then he headed home against Guingamp as well. *GOAL!*

Alex was up to eleven goals in only thirteen Ligue 1 games, and they kept on coming. Two against Thonon Évian, two against Caen, two against Bordeaux, and then two more against Toulouse.

Wow, that was twenty-one goals in twenty games now – incredible! Alex had left Zlatan and Cavani trailing a long way behind. Every time he walked out onto the football pitch, he expected to score, and so did the Lyon fans. When he only got one goal in the next game against Lens, they were a bit disappointed. That's how brilliant their star striker had become.

'Laca's got to be one of the best in the world right now!' they argued proudly.

When Deschamps gave Alex another chance for France, he didn't disappoint. In fact, it only took him thirteen minutes to score against Denmark. As he pounced on a loose ball, he scuffed his shot badly, but he was playing so well that everything he touched still turned into success:

Goooooooooooooooooooooaaaaaaaaaaaaaaaaalllllllllllll llllllllllllll!!!!!!!!!!!!!!!!!!!!

'Come on!' Alex shouted, jumping up to punch the air. It felt so good to be scoring for France too.

'Hey, stop showing off,' Antoine joked, 'otherwise you're going to take my place in the team!'

And Alex's fine form continued when he returned to Lyon. The goals kept going in – *twenty-two, twenty-three, twenty-four, twenty-five…*

…And now twenty-six! With a left-foot volley against Reims, Alex broke the Lyon club record for most goals scored in one season. But even in that magical moment, he still didn't forget about the teammates around him. He wasn't scoring all those goals on his own.

'Thanks for the cross!' Alex cheered, running over to celebrate with Clinton.

Alex finished the season with a terrific total of twenty-seven goals in just thirty-three games. It was time to take a bow because he was the new Ligue 1 top scorer, six goals ahead of André-Pierre Gignac and eight ahead of Zlatan and Cavani.

And that wasn't the only big award that Alex won. Although PSG had beaten Lyon to the Ligue 1 title, there was no doubt who had been the best player that season, with his twenty-seven goals and eight assists...

'Alexandre Lacazette!'

Wearing a smart suit and bowtie, he made his way up onto the stage, as everyone in the room clapped and cheered. Oh boy, look at all those faces! Alex was a superstar on the football pitch now, but off it, he was still the same shy guy that he had always been.

'I am very proud,' Alex said during his short speech. 'Thank you, it is a dream come true to win this trophy.'

So, what next? That was a good question; Alex needed to have a long, hard think about his next move.

'Bro, everyone's talking about you!' Raphaël told him. 'Only two players scored more goals than you last year in the top European leagues – Messi and Ronaldo!'

Alex would always love Lyon, his childhood club, but after such a top-scoring season, was it time to consider signing for a club outside France?

CHAPTER 18

STAYING LOYAL AT LYON

During the summer of 2015, Alex did his best to ignore all of the transfer rumours surrounding him, but it was hard when people kept asking him about them.

'Is it true – are you really about to sign for Arsenal?'

'No!'

'Have Lyon accepted an offer from Liverpool instead?'

'No!'

After thinking long and hard, Alex had decided to stay loyal to his local team, at least for another few years. Thanks to him, Lyon were back in the Champions League, and soon they would be moving

into a brand-new stadium too. The club had made
some high-quality new signings to celebrate those
two facts: right-back Rafael Da Silva from Manchester
United, centre-back Mapou Yanga-Mbiwa from
Roma, and France international playmaker Mathieu
Valbuena from Dynamo Moscow.

So for all those reasons, it was an exciting time for
Lyon, and Alex wanted to be a part of everything.
Plus, he was still only twenty-four years old. There
would be plenty of time to take on a new challenge
later in his career.

'People can stop talking about me now,' Alex
told the media as he signed his new contract. 'Well
actually, they can talk about me scoring goals and
winning games instead!'

'Phew!' the Lyon supporters breathed out a big
sigh of relief. Thank goodness Alex was staying.
What would they have done without their local
hero? The team really relied on their star striker,
especially in the big games like 'Le Derby'.

With twelve games played, Lyon and Saint-Étienne
were tied on twenty-two points each, joint second

in the Ligue 1 table. So this time, the match was even more important than usual. It wasn't just about beating their local rivals; it was also about challenging PSG for the title.

'Come on, let's win this!' the Lyon captain Maxime Gonalons shouted in the dressing room before kick-off.

Standing next to him, the team's other leader stayed quiet. Alex preferred to let his feet do the talking. So far, he had only scored two goals all season, but this was a big game and he was a big game player. At home at the especially loud Stade de Gerland, he was ready to be Lyon's local hero again.

For most of the first half, however, Alex was left looking very frustrated. He wanted to be on the ball causing trouble, but so far, he had barely had a touch, let alone a shot.

All of a sudden, he spotted some confusion in the Saint-Étienne defence. As the ball bounced, one player left it to the other – a big mistake when Lyon's lethal striker was sniffing around! Before the defenders knew what was going on, Alex had stolen the ball and was racing into the penalty area.

'Yes, yes, yes!' the home fans cheered, jumping out of their seats. They knew what was coming next.

As the goalkeeper rushed out and dived at his feet, Alex coolly chipped it over him and into the net.

Gooooooooooooooooooooaaaaaaaaaaaaaaaaaallllllllllllll lllllllllllllll!!!!!!!!!!!!!!!!!!!!

Over by the corner flag, Alex cupped his ear to the crowd as if to say, 'I can't hear you!' The fans responded by making even more noise.

'Wow, I love this club!' Alex thought to himself, feeling glad that he had stayed loyal to Lyon.

There was more magic to come in the second half. When Rafael's shot was saved, Alex pounced on the rebound in a flash.

Gooooooooooooooooooooaaaaaaaaaaaaaaaaaallllllllllllll lllllllllllllll!!!!!!!!!!!!!!!!!!!!

As he slid across the grass on his knees, Alex threw his arms up above his head. Two goals in Le Derby – what a local hero he was! But still, he wasn't satisfied – he always wanted more. In the last minute of the match, Alex ran onto Jordan Ferri's through ball, dribbled around the keeper and passed it into the empty net.

Goooooooooooooooooooaaaaaaaaaaaaaaaaalllllllllllll lllllllllllll!!!!!!!!!!!!!!!!!!

It was party time now, as Alex danced his way back to the halfway line.

Lyon 3 Saint-Étienne 0,

Alex 3 Saint-Étienne 0!

After scoring a hat-trick against their biggest rivals, he wasn't just a Lyon hero anymore; he was now a Lyon legend.

Alexandre Lacazette, Lacazette, Lacazette!

Alexandre Lacazette, woah oah!

At the grand opening of Lyon's new stadium, who scored their opening goal against Troyes? Alex, of course! In the eighteenth minute, he fooled his marker brilliantly and fired a perfect shot into the far corner of the net. *1–0!*

'It had to be you who scored the first goal, didn't it?' Clément said with a smile as Lyon's two academy kids celebrated together.

Those were the highlights of a solid, if not

spectacular, season for Alex.

For him as a striker, twenty-one goals was still a very good total, but it was six fewer than the previous season, and a massive seventeen fewer than the new Ligue 1 top scorer, Zlatan.

'Hey, that guy's a genius!' Alex argued with Clément. He was trying to learn as much as possible from playing against the superstar Swede.

For Lyon as a team, they were pretty pleased to finish second behind PSG in Ligue 1 again, but disappointed with their poor performance in the Champions League. Up against Valencia, Zenit Saint Petersburg and Gent, they should have got through the group stage but instead, they had finished bottom with only one win out of six. And Lyon's star striker had only managed to score two goals in those games.

All in all, it was a simple case of 'MUST DO BETTER' for Alex and his team as they prepared for the 2016–17 season. Alex had narrowly missed out on the France squad for Euro 2016, but he never complained about that, or let it get him down. Instead, he kept working hard in training, using that frustration to inspire him to bigger and better things.

Lyon started the new Ligue 1 season with two wins in a row, and Alex scored all five of their goals. What would they ever do without their local hero? For now, they didn't need to worry because for now, he was there to stay.

One against Guingamp, two against Toulouse…

By Christmas, Alex was already on thirteen Ligue 1 goals, with many more games to go.

… Two against Caen, two against Marseille, two against Montpellier, two against Nice.

Alex's cheeky chip on the last day of the season was his hundredth league goal for Lyon, and his twenty-eighth goal that season, in only thirty appearances. Incredible, he had beaten his previous best scoring record by one! He made it look so easy, but was it *too* easy for him in France?

'Hey, I got seven goals in Europe too!' Alex pointed out to his brothers.

Lyon had been knocked out in the group stage of the Champions League once again, but this time, they had gone into the Europa League instead.

There, they made it all the way to the semi-finals thanks to Alex's great goals: two against AZ Alkmaar, two against Ajax, one against Beşiktaş and, best of all, a long-range rocket against Mohamed Salah's Roma.

In the last minute against Roma, Mathieu passed to Alex on the edge of the penalty area and then kept running forward for the one-two. But Lyon's star striker had other ideas. Before the defenders could get close enough to block it, Alex fired off a ferocious shot that flew straight into the top corner. It was simply unstoppable.

Goooooooooooooooooooaaaaaaaaaaaaaaaalllllllllllll llllllllllllll!!!!!!!!!!!!!!!!!!!

Alex just stood there, totally still and not even smiling, while the other Lyon players went wild around him. He made it look so easy, but again, he was wondering if it was it *too* easy for him in the Europa League as well? Was it time for him to finally leave Lyon and challenge himself at a higher level – in the Champions League and, perhaps, the Premier League?

CHAPTER 19

ARSENAL ATTRACTION

Newcastle United, Tottenham, Manchester United, Liverpool, West Ham – Alex was now wanted by most of the teams in England. They all thought he, with his pace, power and sensational scoring record, would be perfect for the Premier League. However, one club above all had been watching Alex's progress, and they had been doing so for ten long years: Arsenal.

Yes, way back in 2007, their manager, Arsène Wenger, sent his French scout, Gilles Grimandi, to watch Lyon's latest academy stars. Grimandi had been impressed by Clément and Yannis, but it was Alex who really stood out. Even at the age of just sixteen, he already had the quiet confidence of a superstar. Plus, he was scoring goals for fun.

'Alexandre Lacazette – he looks like the real deal!' the Arsenal scout reported back to his manager.

Wenger watched Alex in action, but in the end, he decided to wait. Because although Thierry Henry had just left to join Barcelona, Arsenal still had a strong group of strikers: Emmanuel Adebayor, Robin van Persie, Eduardo, Nicklas Bendtner, Theo Walcott, Carlos Vela... And for the future, Arsenal already had Gilles Sunu, who played with Alex in the France Under-17s.

'Let's just keep an eye on Lacazette for now,' Wenger told his scout.

But after Alex's performances at the Under-17 and Under-19 European Championships, Arsenal were no longer the only club watching him. He was attracting interest from all the top teams.

'Don't you think we should sign him now?' Grimandi asked his manager. 'Before someone else does?'

But Wenger still wasn't sure. He liked Alex, but was he really the right player for Arsenal? Did he have that star quality like Henry? Only time would tell, and The Gunners needed a striker who could shine straight away.

So in 2010, they signed Marouane Chamakh from Bordeaux, in 2011, they signed Gervinho from Lille, in 2012, they signed Olivier Giroud from Montpellier, and in 2013, they signed Yaya Sanogo from Toulouse.

At that stage, Alex had just scored four goals in a whole season. It looked like Wenger had been right to wait and see about Lyon's young star. But after his talk with Thierry, Alex had turned himself into the super-striker that Grimandi had predicted he would be all those years earlier.

Twenty-two goals, then thirty-one, then thirty-three, then thirty-seven...

'Okay, now we have to sign him!' Wenger decided. Alex had proved that he did have the star quality to shine at Arsenal.

This time, there wasn't a moment to wait. Alex had offers from other Premier League clubs, but also from Atlético Madrid in Spain and Borussia

Dortmund in Germany. So, Arsenal would need to work extra hard to sign him. During the summer, Wenger travelled to France to discuss a deal with Alex over dinner.

'You're the star striker that we've been waiting for!' the Arsenal manager told him enthusiastically. 'We can't offer you Champions League football this season, but I'm confident that you can get us back there next year. Playing with Mesut Özil and Alexis Sánchez, you're going to be scoring all the time!'

That was a very tempting idea indeed. Arsenal played the game Alex's favourite way, with lots of passing and moving, and beautiful, flowing football. Wenger was right; Alex plus Özil plus Alexis would surely equal goals galore!

Plus, Alex had always loved Arsenal, ever since he was a young boy in the Lyon academy, during the glory days of Henry and The Invincibles. And although the team wasn't winning as many trophies anymore, he could hopefully help fire them back to the top.

'Let's do this,' Alex told his agent.

It was going to be a giant step for Alex, the biggest of his life so far. Not only was he leaving Lyon, his local club, but he would also be leaving his friends and family. He would no longer be able to go around to his parents' house for his mum's Colombo Chicken dinner whenever he liked. But Alex was twenty-six now; the timing was right to test himself in the Premier League, the most exciting league in the world.

At last, Wenger had got his star striker, but Lyon weren't going to let their local hero go cheaply. Eventually, the two clubs agreed a fee of £46.5 million, rising to £52 million if he did well. Alex was officially Arsenal's new record signing, with a lot to live up to.

'They're the club that plays the best football in England, so I really wanted to come here,' he told the media, proudly holding up his new red-and-white shirt for the cameras. 'And thanks to Thierry Henry, I always dreamed of playing for this club when I was young.'

Alex was nervous but also excited about his

Arsenal challenge. After all those years at his hometown team, suddenly everything was brand new – the club, the country, *and* the language.

'Now I wish I hadn't skipped so many English classes at school to go and play football!' he joked with his brothers.

'Don't worry, most of the Arsenal players are French anyway!' Benoît laughed.

Alex knew Olivier Giroud, Laurent Koscielny and Mathieu Debuchy from the France national team. And he also had one old friend at the club who he had known for even longer, almost as long as Arsenal had been scouting him.

'You're finally here!' Francis Coquelin cheered, giving him a great big hug.

Alex and Francis had played together for the France Under-19s, Under-20s *and* Under-21s. For years, Francis had been trying to persuade Alex to come to England, and to Arsenal in particular.

'You'll love it here, mate! It's a great club, the fans are amazing, and London is a really cool city to live in.'

Well, Francis's plan had worked because yes, Alex was now finally here! After the press conference, he walked around the Emirates, thinking back to his first time at the stadium in 2010. That day, everything had been a blur. Alex and Francis had returned from winning the Under-19 Euros with France just in time to play for their clubs in the preseason Emirates Cup.

Alex starred in two games in two days for Lyon, but never dreamed that one day, the Arsenal stadium would be his new home.

'Just look at me now!' Alex said to himself as a big smile spread across his face.

CHAPTER 20

LOVING LIFE IN THE PREMIER LEAGUE

Alex's debut Arsenal season started with success straight away in August 2017, as the Gunners beat Chelsea on penalties in the Community Shield.

'I think I'm going to like it here!' he joked with Olivier as they lifted the trophy together at Wembley.

But Alex's main focus was the Premier League. He had heard so many things about the pace and physicality of English football, and he couldn't wait to experience it for himself.

For Arsenal's first game of the 2017–18 season against Leicester City, Wenger started Alex in attack with Mesut Özil and Danny Welbeck. It turned out to be a debut that he would never, ever forget.

Walking out of the tunnel at the Emirates,
Alex felt like he was in a different football world.
Everything felt brighter and louder and more
exciting.

…Come on, Arsenal!

…I'm Arsenal till I die!

…We love you Arsenal, we do!

It was Alex who kicked the game off, and less
than two minutes later, he was celebrating his first
Premier League goal.

On the right wing, Héctor Bellerín played it back
to Mohamed Elneny, who curled a lovely cross into
the box. The ball flew past the Leicester centre-backs
and straight onto Alex's head. With a powerful flick,
he guided it past Kasper Schmeichel and into the
bottom corner. *1–0!*

*Goooooooooooooooooooooaaaaaaaaaaaaaaaaalllllllllllll
llllllllllllll!!!!!!!!!!!!!!!!!!!!!*

As the Arsenal fans went wild, Alex just stood
there in front of them with his arms out wide as if to
say, 'Yeah, that's what I can do!'

'What a header!' Danny shouted, jumping on his

back. 'Welcome to the Premier League!'

But only three minutes later, Leicester were level, and the game just got crazier and crazier.

Jamie Vardy tapped in at the back-post. *2–1 to Leicester!*

Alex used his strength to turn brilliantly in the box. He slipped and scuffed his shot, but Danny was there to bundle the ball in. *2–2!*

Game on! But early in the second half, Vardy headed in from a corner. *3–2 to Leicester!*

Uh oh, Arsenal were heading for a disastrous home defeat. So, Wenger brought on Olivier and Aaron Ramsey. Could they be the super subs?

Yes! Aaron snuck in at the back post to score the equaliser. *3–3!*

A minute later, Alex dribbled into the Leicester penalty area and forced Schmeichel to make a super save. From the corner, Olivier jumped up and headed the ball home. *4–3 to Arsenal!*

'Yesssss!' Alex cheered, throwing his arms up in the air and chasing after his teammate.

At the full-time whistle, Arsenal were the winners

and Alex had his first goal and his first taste of
exciting English football.

'Wow, I love the Premier League already!' he said
to Olivier.

Alex had made the Emirates his home
immediately. He could tell that he was going to have
lots of fun there, in front of Arsenal's amazing fans.
In the next home game against Bournemouth, he
played a nice one-two with Danny and then sent an
unstoppable shot sailing towards the top corner.

*Goooooooooooooooooooooaaaaaaaaaaaaaaaaaalllllllllllll
lllllllllllllll!!!!!!!!!!!!!!!!!!!!*

Two goals in two games! Alex jumped up and
punched the air. Soon he would need to start scoring
away-goals too, but for now, he was just enjoying life
at the Emirates.

West Brom were the next visitors and Arsenal's
new record signing welcomed them in similar style.
When Alexis's free kick crashed back off the crossbar,
Alex was the first to react. He raced in like a classic
striker to head home the rebound.

Goooooooooooooooooooooaaaaaaaaaaaaaaaaaalllllllllllll

IIIIIIIIIIIIIIIII!!!!!!!!!!!!!!!!!!!!!!!

In the second half, Alex added a penalty kick to his Premier League total. That made it four goals in his first three home games.

'Arsenal have certainly found themselves a new scorer this season!' said the commentator on TV.

Alex's manager was really impressed with how quickly he had settled into his new team. 'He is young and just arrived in England, but he's getting stronger in every game,' Wenger praised his striker.

Yes, despite his strong start, Alex believed that his best was still to come. Premier League defences, beware! Not even Thierry Henry had scored in his first three home league matches for Arsenal. So, what next? An away goal, perhaps?

At Goodison Park, Arsenal fought back from 1–0 down to lead Everton 2–1. They were playing the kind of beautiful, flowing football that Alex loved most, but could he add his name to the scoresheet? After his dramatic debut against Leicester, he knew that Arsenal needed at least one more goal before they could feel safe about the victory.

'Yes, over here!'

As Mesut raced down the right on a quick counterattack, Alex was waiting in the middle, calling for the ball. If the pass arrived, he knew that he would score – it was that simple in his mind. In fact, after his strong start at Arsenal, Alex was feeling so confident that he decided to shoot first time.

Gooooooooooooooooooooaaaaaaaaaaaaaaaaaallllllllllll llllllllllllllll!!!!!!!!!!!!!!!!!!!!

'Thanks, Mesut!' he shouted, running over to hug his partner in attack. Scoring was always so much easier when he had awesome teammates around him.

Alex's next challenge was scoring a big game goal. So far that season, Arsenal had lost 4–0 to Liverpool, and drawn 0–0 at Chelsea. They would need to do better than that if they wanted to achieve their target of getting back into the Champions League.

Away at league leaders Manchester City, Alex came on for his friend Francis early in the second half. By then, Arsenal were already 2–0 down and in desperate need of a super sub.

'That's going to be me!' he told himself
determinedly.

Alex hadn't been on the pitch for long when
he raced onto Aaron's pass. He took one touch to
control it, another to dribble into the box and then a
third to fire the ball through Ederson's legs. *2–1!*

*Goooooooooooooooooooooaaaaaaaaaaaaaaaaalllllllllllll
llllllllllllll!!!!!!!!!!!!!!!!!!!*

What a fantastic finish! These days, Alex never
missed a scoring chance like that. He was a stone-
cold striker like his hero Henry.

'Come on!' Alex called out to his Arsenal
teammates as they ran back for the restart. Thanks to
their super sub, they were back in the game.

For now. Nine minutes later, Manchester City
made it 3–1. That was the thing about the Premier
League; games could change so quickly. It was one of
the many reasons that Alex already loved it.

CHAPTER 21

BOUNCING BACK FROM INJURY

By January 2018, Arsenal were stuck in sixth position in the Premier League, five points off fourth place, that final Champions League spot.

'Come on, we can still do this!' the club captain, Laurent, urged his teammates.

But the Arsenal owners decided that it was time for some big changes. First, Alexis went to Manchester United in a swap deal with Henrikh Mkhitaryan. And then on transfer deadline day, the club signed Pierre-Emerick Aubameyang from Borussia Dortmund for £56 million.

That was an extraordinary price for a new star striker! Suddenly, Alex was no longer the club's record signing, and he was no longer a guaranteed starter either. He knew all about 'Auba' because he had played for Lyon's local rivals, Saint-Étienne. Pierre-Emerick was super-speedy and a great goalscorer too.

'But what about me?' Alex wanted to ask Wenger.

What had he done wrong? Alex had scored nine goals in his first twenty-seven games. No, that wasn't anywhere near as good as his amazing record at Lyon, but as the Arsenal manager himself had said, he was still getting stronger all the time.

'Maybe he'll pick both of us and play us together as strike partners!' Alex thought hopefully.

But in the next match against Everton, it was Auba who started and Alex who stayed on the bench. And for the big North London derby against Tottenham, Alex only came on for the last twenty-five minutes when Arsenal were losing.

'I don't get it,' he said as he discussed it with his dad on the phone. 'Why can't Auba and I just play in the same team? I'll bring the strength and he can bring the speed. We would score so many goals together!'

That idea would have to wait, however, because Alex had a bad knee injury. He had been playing through the pain for weeks now, but he could feel it getting worse and worse. He had to stop and sort it out, even if it meant surgery and six weeks without football.

'Noooooooo!' Alex groaned when the Arsenal team doctor delivered the news.

Six whole weeks? He looked at the fixture list – that meant that he would miss at least three Premier League games, the Europa League Last 16, and worst of all, the EFL Cup Final against Manchester City!

Oh well, all Alex could do was work hard on his recovery and cheer on his team. 'Come on, you Gunners!'

But without him, Arsenal lost 3–0 to Manchester City in the cup final, then 3–0 to Manchester City in the league, and then 2–1 away at Brighton too.

Uh oh, that fourth Champions League spot was slipping further and further away from them...

Alex pushed himself harder and harder in the gym,

building up the strength in his knee again. Arsenal needed him to be fit and firing as soon as possible.

'Back to training with my teammates,' he told his Twitter followers in late March.

Hurray! By the start of April, Alex was ready to make his return at last. When he came on to replace Danny Welbeck against Stoke, it was 0–0 with thirty minutes to go. Perfect! It was all set up for him to be the Arsenal hero and show Wenger how well he could play alongside Auba.

He ran and ran, hunting for even the smallest chance to score. With Alex, Auba and Mesut in the same attack, Arsenal looked so much more dangerous. When Héctor headed the ball across, Alex wriggled his way into the six-yard box, but his shot was blocked.

'Come on!' he shouted, picking himself up and carrying on.

Finally, Arsenal got the goal they were looking for. Alex flicked the ball through to Mesut, who was fouled as he dribbled into the area. Penalty! Auba scored from the spot. *1–0!*

'Great work!' Alex cheered, high-fiving his new strike partner.

After that, it was all Arsenal. Auba scored a second goal and then Alex was pushed as he went to shoot. Another penalty!

'You won it, you take it,' Auba said, handing him the ball, even though he was on a hat-trick.

'Thanks, mate!'

Alex stepped up confidently and sent the keeper the wrong way. *3–0!*

Goooooooooooooooooooaaaaaaaaaaaaaaaaalllllllllllll llllllllllllll!!!!!!!!!!!!!!!!!!!

As he threw his arms out wide, Auba was the first to come over and congratulate him.

'Welcome back, Laca – we've really missed you!'

Alex was so pleased to be playing football again.

'What a feeling to be back at home,' he wrote on social media. 'Thanks to all the fans for the support!'

As soon as the Stoke match finished, Alex was looking forward to the next one. Fortunately for him, Arsenal's Europa League quarter-final against CSKA Moscow was only four days away. And with Auba cup-tied, Alex had to be his team's star striker.

No problem! It turned out to be another excellent night at the Emirates.

Aaron finished off a marvellous team move. *1–0!*

Alex scored from the penalty spot. *2–1!*

Aaron lobbed the keeper with a brilliant flick. *3–1!*

Alex controlled Mesut's cross and fired a left-footed shot into the bottom corner. *4–1!*

'What a strike, Laca!' Héctor cheered happily.

Arsenal's top scorer was back with a bang, so was now the time for that Alex and Auba strike partnership? That's what the fans were desperate to see. Wenger still preferred playing one or the other, but whenever they were both on the pitch at the same time together, they were so exciting to watch.

Alex slid in at the back post to volley home Auba's cross against Newcastle. *GOAL!*

Auba thought about shooting in the West Ham box, but he passed to Alex instead. *GOAL!*

Auba slid in at the back post to tap home Alex's cross against Burnley. *GOAL!*

Alex finished his first season in England with

seventeen goals, and his new best friend wasn't far behind on ten. The fans loved watching the 'Auba and Laca' show, and it was only just getting started. Arsenal had failed to qualify for the Champions League this time, but next year? Anything seemed possible with their next star strikeforce.

CHAPTER 22

AUBA AND LACA

'Merci, Arsène!'

At the end of the 2017–18 season, there were more big changes at Arsenal. After an incredible twenty-two years in charge of the club, Wenger had decided to say goodbye. Their new manager, Unai Emery, had very big boots to fill.

'I'm very excited to be starting this important new chapter in Arsenal's history,' the Spanish coach said.

Alex was very sad to see Wenger leave. After all, he was the man who had watched him for ten years before finally signing him for Arsenal. He would always be grateful for that. But at the same time, Alex felt excited about the future. It was time to move forward, and maybe Emery would let 'Auba and Laca' play together more often.

'We'll just have to show him that we're the perfect pair!' Pierre-Emerick laughed, putting his arm around Alex.

But no, when the new season started, Auba was up front and Alex was on the bench. Again.

'I don't want to be a super sub,' Alex grumbled after a 3–2 defeat at Chelsea. 'I want to be a super starter!'

It was easy to see that Arsenal were a better team with both of their star strikers on the pitch together.

Alex came on at half-time against West Ham, with the score at 1–1. Twenty-five minutes later, he chested the ball down brilliantly, used his strength to hold off his marker, and then fired the ball in off Auba. *2–1 to Arsenal!*

'Come on!' Alex screamed, throwing his arms around and letting out all that frustration.

That was enough to make Emery change his mind. In the next game against Cardiff City, the Arsenal manager played all of his best attackers in the same team from the start.

Mesut passed to Alex, who flicked the ball cleverly through to Pierre-Emerick, who shot into the top corner. *2–1!*

Auba and Laca danced their way towards each other, with huge smiles on their faces. They were having so much fun together for Arsenal.

With time running out, Lucas Torreira slipped the ball through to Alex in the box. His first touch was perfect, as he swivelled his body and *BANG!* No-one could turn and shoot like Laca. The ball was in the back of the net before the Cardiff keeper could even react. *3–2!*

Goooooooooooooooooooooaaaaaaaaaaaaaaaaalllllllllllll llllllllllllll!!!!!!!!!!!!!!!!!!!!

It was another winning goal for Alex, and what a beauty! This time, there was a lot less emotion in his celebration. Instead, he just coolly danced his way over to the corner flag.

Suddenly, Arsenal were on fire, winning game after game. On their own, Alex and Pierre-Emerick were both brilliant strikers, but together, they were simply unstoppable. They scored one each against

Everton, and then two each against Fulham. Auba scored the goals to beat Leicester City and then Laca grabbed the late equaliser against Liverpool. With eleven games played, Arsenal were in fourth place, that final Champions League spot.

'Now, we've just got to stay here!' Emery urged his team.

Luckily, his star strikers had saved their best for the big North London derby. At half-time at the Emirates, Tottenham were winning 2–1, so the Arsenal manager sent on Alex and Aaron. What a double substitution!

Aaron set up Pierre-Emerick, who curled the ball into the top corner. *2–2!*

Then Alex dribbled towards the goal with two defenders in front of him. Even though he slipped as he shot with his weaker left foot, his accuracy was still amazing. The ball skidded past his old Lyon teammate Hugo Lloris and into the bottom corner. *3–2!*

Goooooooooooooooooooaaaaaaaaaaaaaaaalllllllllllll llllllllllllll!!!!!!!!!!!!!!!!!!!

157

Another game, another winning goal from Alex. As it went in, the Arsenal supporters went wild, and so did their players. It was an incredible comeback, and especially in a North London derby. Alex slid towards the corner flag on his knees, with all of his teammates right behind him.

'Laca, I love you, man!' Pierre-Emerick screamed in his ear.

Their friendship was growing stronger and stronger. Alex was quiet, whereas Pierre-Emerick was loud; Alex often looked very serious, whereas Pierre-Emerick was always smiling. But despite their different characters, they had a lot in common. They both loved music and basketball, and on the football pitch, they both loved to entertain.

Arsenal's BFFs were now everyone's favourite partnership in the Premier League. Not only did Auba and Laca score lots of great goals together, they also performed lots of great goal celebrations: the knee slide, the happy dance, and best of all, the special handshake.

It had started away at Cardiff City, when Alex

scored the winning goal. They performed their old celebration, bowing at each other and then shaking hands like old-fashioned gentleman.

'Well done, sir!'

Everyone loved it, and so after that, they did it every time one of them scored. Wow – that was a lot of goals and a lot of special handshakes!

In December, Alex set up three for Pierre-Emerick and Henrikh. Then in January, it was his turn to score. That month, Alex's goals got better and better. First, a tap-in against Fulham, then a classic turn-and-shoot against Chelsea, and finally, a sensational solo strike against Cardiff.

The latter all started with a simple pass from Pierre-Emerick near the halfway line. Alex was out wide on the right wing, but he skipped past one tackle and then burst forward at top speed, dribbling all the way into the box. With a quick look up, he fired a shot into the far corner. *2–0!*

Gooooooooooooooooooooaaaaaaaaaaaaaaaaalllllllllllll llllllllllllll!!!!!!!!!!!!!!!!!!!!!!

'Okay, you win, Laca – your goal was better!'

Pierre-Emerick laughed. His had been a simple penalty.

Alex's goalscoring form was so good that he was named on the shortlist for the Premier League Player of the Month, and he followed that up with three more in February. That took him to twelve goals for the season, only three behind Pierre-Emerick.

'You better watch your back, Auba – I'm coming for you!'

Unfortunately, Alex only managed one more Premier League goal after that, but there were plenty more to come in the Europa League, where Arsenal were flying towards the final. After winning their group, they beat BATE Borisov and then French club Stade Rennais.

'Come on, you Gunners!'

After a reckless red card against BATE Borisov, Alex was eager to make up for his mistake. He had let his team down, and so now he needed to put things right by firing Arsenal into the semi-finals and beyond. Standing in their way, however, were the Italian giants Napoli. They had lots of top players

like Lorenzo Insigne, Dries Mertens and Kalidou
Koulibaly. It wouldn't be easy to beat them, but Alex
was determined.

As the match kicked off at the San Paolo Stadium,
the atmosphere was tense and unwelcoming. Arsenal
had won the first leg 2–0 at the Emirates, but Napoli
were so strong at home. An away goal was what The
Gunners needed to calm the nerves...

Midway through the first half, Alex battled for the
ball and won a free kick near the Napoli penalty area.
Granit Xhaka wanted to take it, but Alex had a better
idea.

'I've got this,' he told his teammate confidently.
And with a very short run-up, Alex curled the ball up
over the wall and into the top corner.

*Goooooooooooooooooooaaaaaaaaaaaaaaaalllllllllll
llllllllllllll!!!!!!!!!!!!!!!!!!!*

'Yes, Laca!' the Arsenal players screamed, jumping
joyfully on their hero. Alex was delighted with his
free kick; now, he felt like he had made up for his
mistake.

That goal was enough to take them through to

a semi-final against Valencia. Alex would be going head-to-head with his friend and former Arsenal teammate, Francis. In the week before the game, they sent each other funny messages, but once matchday arrived, they were both fully focused on winning.

The previous season, Arsenal had lost to Atlético Madrid in the semi-finals. This time, though, the players were full of belief because Auba and Laca were too hot for any defence to handle. Alex slipped the ball through to Pierre-Emerick and then carried on his run. As he arrived on the edge of the Valencia penalty area, Pierre-Emerick passed it back to his best friend.

Goooooooooooooooooooaaaaaaaaaaaaaaaaalllllllllll llllllllllllll!!!!!!!!!!!!!!!!!!

'Thanks, Auba!' Alex shouted, pointing at his strike partner.

The entire football world was enjoying their wonderful teamwork, including his good friend Antoine Griezmann. 'Lacazette – what a player!' he tweeted proudly.

Alex scored a second goal with a header, and then Pierre-Emerick added a third with a volley. At 3–1, surely Arsenal were on their way to the Europa League final? But just to make sure, their star strikeforce scored four more goals in the second leg. Auba and Laca even showed off a brand-new celebration – the ice-cold shiver dance.

'Let's go to the final!' Alex posted on social media, with a picture of the Arsenal team celebrating together in the dressing room.

He had already shown that he was a big game player – for the France youth teams, Lyon and for Arsenal – but this was the new biggest game of his career so far. And Alex couldn't wait for it to begin.

'Come on, we've got to win that trophy!'

Their opponents in the Europa League final were London rivals Chelsea. They had Eden Hazard and Olivier in attack, but Arsenal had Auba and Laca.

Early in the first half, Pierre-Emerick flicked a clever header into Alex's path. He was too quick for César Azpilicueta, but what about the Chelsea keeper, who was rushing out of his goal? Alex got to the ball just before Kepa, but as he tried to dribble around him, he felt that he was tripped.

'Penalty!' Alex cried out as his body rolled across the grass.

But after checking with VAR, the referee said no.

'What?' Alex threw his head back in frustration. He couldn't believe it, and neither could Pierre-Emerick. But all they could do was get on with the game, and work together to create another chance...

Sadly, it just wasn't Alex's, or Arsenal's, night. Shots went wide and passes went wrong. After a long season, the team looked tired and Hazard took full advantage in the second half: *1–0, 2–0, 3–0!* Alex Iwobi pulled one goal back for Arsenal, but then Chelsea scored again.

In the last few seconds, Alex had a great chance to score. He controlled the cross well, but then the ball got stuck under his feet. 'Nooooo!' he groaned as a defender cleared it away. It summed up his disappointing night.

After the final whistle, Alex sat there, sad and alone in the Chelsea penalty area, wondering: What if that penalty had been awarded? What if he had done things differently each time he touched the ball? But it was too late to think like that; Arsenal would just have to bounce back and reach the final again next year.

Alex ended his second season at the club without a team trophy, and without Champions League to look forward to either. But he did have one individual award to enjoy. The supporters had selected him as the Arsenal Player of the Year!

Nineteen goals and thirteen assists – Alex was very proud of his improvement. Life hadn't always been easy in England since his brave move away from Lyon, but all that hard work had paid off. Alongside Auba, Alex was now showing his real star quality in Arsenal's attack. And if he kept shining, maybe he could still make his World Cup dream come true.

Lyon

🏆 Coupe de France: 2011–12

🏆 Trophée des Champions: 2012

Arsenal

🏆 FA Community Shield: 2017

France Youth

🏆 UEFA European Under-19 Championship: 2010

Individual

🏆 UNFP Ligue 1 Team of the Year: 2013–14, 2014–15, 2016–17

🏆 UNFP Ligue 1 Player of the Year: 2014–15

🏆 Ligue 1 top scorer: 2014–15

🏆 UEFA Europa League Squad of the Season: 2016–17

🏆 Arsenal Player of the Season: 2018–19

LACAZETTE

9 THE FACTS

NAME: ALEXANDRE LACAZETTE

DATE OF BIRTH: 28 May 1991

AGE: 28

PLACE OF BIRTH: Lyon

NATIONALITY: French

BEST FRIEND: Pierre-Emerick Aubameyang

CURRENT CLUB: Arsenal

POSITION: ST

THE STATS

Height (cm):	175
Club appearances:	388
Club goals:	173
Club trophies:	3
International appearances:	16
International goals:	3
International trophies:	0
Ballon d'Ors:	0

★ ★ ★ **HERO RATING: 84** ★ ★ ★

GREATEST MOMENTS

30 JULY 2010,
SPAIN 1–2 FRANCE

Alex's volley against Ireland at the 2008 Under-17
Euros was a better goal, but this one two years later
at the Under-19 Euros was more important. France
were drawing 1–1 with Spain in the final, when Alex
came on and saved the day. Just when it looked like
the game was going to extra time, France's super sub
snuck in to score the winning goal.

8 NOVEMBER 2015, LYON 3–0 SAINT-ÉTIENNE

As a local boy, Alex knew how important 'Le Derby' against Saint-Étienne was for Lyon supporters. So scoring this hat-trick in a 3–0 win must have been one of the best nights of his life. The goals were good too, including a cheeky chip over the keeper.

9 MARCH 2017, LYON 4–2 ROMA

This Europa League wonderstrike was all about technique. In the last minute against Mohamed Salah's Roma, Alex got the ball just outside the box. In a flash, he fired off a ferocious shot that flew straight into the top corner. Alex was already a star in France, but now he was starting to shine in Europe too.

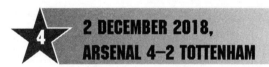

2 DECEMBER 2018,
ARSENAL 4–2 TOTTENHAM

Alex was Arsenal's super sub in this famous North
London derby fightback. He came on at half-time
and helped change the game completely. His strike
partner Pierre-Emerick scored the equaliser and then
Alex scored the winner with a perfectly aimed shot
into the bottom corner.

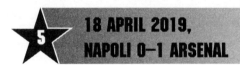

18 APRIL 2019,
NAPOLI 0–1 ARSENAL

Alex hasn't scored many free kicks in his career, but
this was an absolute beauty. Against Napoli in the
Europa League quarter-final, Arsenal were looking for
an away goal. So up stepped Alex to curl the ball over
the wall and into the top corner. He also starred in
Arsenal's semi-final win against Valencia, only to be
beaten by Chelsea in the final.

PLAY LIKE YOUR HEROES

TURN AND SHOOT LIKE LACA

Step 1: Always stay alert up front. You never know when your team is going to break away on the attack.

Step 2: When they do, use your speed to burst into the box, and then call for the ball.

Step 3: When it arrives, take a nice first touch and use your strength to hold off your marker.

Step 4: Right now, you've got your back to goal, but that's okay because you're going to swivel your body around in an instant.

Step 5: Ta-da! Before the defender can make the block, shoot powerfully and accurately past the keeper.

Step 6: GOAL! If you've got an awesome strike partner like Auba, then do a special celebration with them. If not, just do a cool dance on your own and wait for your teammates to join in.

TEST YOUR KNOWLEDGE

QUESTIONS

1. Other than as striker, what position did Alex like to play at Elan Sportif?

2. Why did Alex stop playing that position?

3. Which English club did Alex support as a kid and why?

4. Who were the other two main stars of Alex's academy team at Lyon?

5. How old was Alex when he made his first-team debut for Lyon?

6. How many goals did Alex score for France at the 2011 Under-20 World Cup?

7. Alex set up Lyon's winning goal in the 2012 Coupe de France final, but who scored it?

8. Only two players scored more goals than Alex in Europe's top leagues during the 2014–15 season. Who were they?

9. Which Arsenal player helped persuade Alex to move to London?

10. How long did it take Alex to score on his Premier League debut?

11. How many World Cups and Euro Championships has Alex played in for France?

Answers below. . . No cheating!

1. Goalkeeper. 2. Because his mum said it was too dangerous! 3. Arsenal, because his hero Thierry Henry played for them. 4. Yannis Tafer and Clément Grenier. 5. Eighteen – it was just before his nineteenth birthday. 6. Five – he was the tournament's joint top scorer. 7. Lisandro López. 8. Ronaldo and Messi. 9. Francis Coquelin. 10. Less than two minutes! 11. Zero! But he was on the standby list for the 2014 and 2018 World Cups and Euro 2016.